Africa and the Metaphysical Empire

This book investigates whether African cultures can appropriate some useful aspects of Western cultures, or whether doing so risks falling into the metaphysical empire and diluting African identity.

Ngugi wa Thiong'o and Ndlovu-Gatsheni characterise the metaphysical empire as an intangible non-physical and non-geographical invasion of the mental universe of formerly colonised peoples. As mutual exclusivists, they argue that authentic decolonization necessitates a complete dissociation of the African and her culture from colonial heritage. However, cultural appropriationists such as Wole Soyinka, Chinua Achebe and Chimamanda Ngozi Adichie argue that the African adoption of colonial heritage such as the English language is in no way antithetical to decolonization. This book delves into the debate by exploring the strengths and weaknesses of cultural appropriationism and, on the other hand, testing the validity of mutual exclusivism. The book demonstrates that cultural appropriation without falling into the metaphysical empire is possible, but that this poses important questions about the nature of the decolonization project itself, and where it should start and stop. A more accommodative decolonization would recognize the relationship between cultural universals and particulars, whilst also creating room for cultural appropriation. Ultimately, the book argues that both cultural appropriationists and mutual exclusivists must simultaneously renounce absolutism. By being amenable to a fusion of horizons, discourse can move beyond the decolonization fallacy of arguing that things are always either/or.

This original and important contribution to the metaphysical empire debate will be a seminal read for researchers across the fields of philosophy, political science, African studies, and Black studies.

Frank Aragbonfoh Abumere is a Visiting Assistant Professor at Clark Atlanta University and a fellow/member of The Abuja School. He has previously been a Senior Member of St Antony's College, University of Oxford and a visiting fellow at both the LSE and the African Studies Centre, University of Oxford. He was also a visiting professor at Vita-Salute San Raffaele University (Milan, Italy), University of Richmond (USA) and University of Montreal (Canada). He is interested in African and African diaspora issues across the fields of philosophy, political science, African studies, and Black studies.

Routledge Studies in African Philosophy

The *Routledge Studies in African Philosophy* book series reflects the many exciting and diverse contributions to philosophy which are being made by Africans and the African diaspora. Historically dominated by the voices of Western thinkers, the field of philosophy is rapidly diversifying and there is a pressing need to reflect on the rich epistemic traditions and history to be found within Africa. Covering all aspects of philosophy, including but not limited to metaphysics, epistemology, moral philosophy, ethnophilosophy, ethics, and political philosophy, this series aims to reflect all regions across the continent and the diaspora.

Intercultural Thinking in African Philosophy
A Critical Dialogue with Kant and Foucault
Marita Rainsborough

Endangered African Knowledges and the Challenge of Modernity
An Igbo Response
Donald Mark C. Ude

Ubuntu Ethics
Human Dignity, Moral Perfectionism, and Needs
Motsamai Molefe

Beyond Decolonial African Philosophy
Africanity, Afrotopia, and Transcolonial Perspectives
Edited by Joseph C. A. Agbakoba and Marita Rainsborough

Africa and the Metaphysical Empire
Frank Aragbonfoh Abumere

For more information about this series, please visit: https://www.routledge.com/Routledge-Studies-in-African-Philosophy/book-series/AFRPHIL

Africa and the Metaphysical Empire

Frank Aragbonfoh Abumere

LONDON AND NEW YORK

First published 2025
by Routledge
4 Park Square, Milton Park, Abingdon, Oxon OX14 4RN

and by Routledge
605 Third Avenue, New York, NY 10158

Routledge is an imprint of the Taylor & Francis Group, an informa business

British Library Cataloguing-in-Publication Data
A catalogue record for this book is available from the British Library

ISBN: 978-1-032-96540-6 (hbk)
ISBN: 978-1-032-96541-3 (pbk)
ISBN: 978-1-003-58983-9 (ebk)

DOI: 10.4324/9781003589839

Typeset in Times New Roman
by SPi Technologies India Pvt Ltd (Straive)

Contents

1 Introduction

What Is the Metaphysical Empire? The Scope and Content of the Metaphysical Empire

What Is the Metaphysical Empire?

In this book, beginning with this chapter, I shall explain in detail what the metaphysical empire is, and what its scope and content are. In a novel way, I shall juxtapose the physical empire with the metaphysical empire, and extend the domain of the metaphysical empire beyond its usual linguistic domain. In this introductory chapter, I shall preliminarily explore the place of the metaphysical empire in the decolonisation project, and the extent to which the project should or should not be concerned with the metaphysical empire.

The simplest way to understand the metaphysical empire is to understand it as Empire 2.0. This goes beyond merely saying what the metaphysical empire 'is.' It goes as far as adopting *via negativa* as a methodological device to say what the metaphysical empire 'is not.' This entails contrasting the tangible physical geographical empire with the intangible non-physical and non-geographical metaphysical empire. In this sense, while we see the tangible physical geographical empire as Empire 1.0, we see the intangible non-physical and non-geographical metaphysical empire as Empire 2.0.

The concept of the metaphysical empire is a pointer to the metamorphosis or transformation of imperialism and empire. For some people, this metamorphosis or transformation is only an idea or a mere conjecture. But for others, it is a fact and reality. Whether an idea or reality, conjecture or fact, there is a palpable perception that imperialism and empire have metamorphosed or have been transformed from Empire 1.0 to Empire 2.0.

In comparison with historical or past imperialism, contemporary or present imperialism has a different scope and content even though both the former and the latter have the same essence. As Atilio B. Boron (2005) said nearly two decades ago, current imperialism is different from the imperialism that existed half a century ago. According to Boron (2005), imperialism has:

DOI: 10.4324/9781003589839-1

> changed, and in some ways the change has been important, but it has not changed into its opposite, as neo-liberal mystification suggests, giving rise to a 'global' economy in which we are all 'interdependent.' It still exists, and it still oppresses people and nations and creates pain, destruction and death. In spite of the changes, it still keeps its identity and structure, and it still plays the same historical role in the logic of the global accumulation of capital. Its mutations, its volatile and dangerous combinations of persistence and innovation, require the construction of a new framework that will allow us to capture its present nature.
>
> (p. 3) (emphasis in original)

Bello's description of empire as an oppressive phenomenon aligns with the thought of many people that empire was or is an evil, and as such, it was or is morally unjustifiable. But among others, the British-American historian Niall Ferguson thinks that empire was a civilising and progressive phenomenon rather than a dehumanising and oppressive phenomenon. These empire apologists argue that empire was good rather than evil, and that Europeans did Africans, Asians, South Americans, North Americans, Central Americans and the people of Caribbean a favour rather than a disservice by colonising them.

Empire apologists' justification of empire is sufficient hint that some people are nostalgic about Empire 1.0. If some people are nostalgic about Empire 1.0, then it should not surprise anyone that Empire 2.0 exists in spite of many peoples' conception of empire as a morally unjustifiable evil and oppressive phenomenon.

The actuality, or at least the possibility of the intersection between Empire 1.0 and Empire 2.0, is aptly captured by Michael Hardt and Antonio Negri (2000) when they say that 'the concept of the Empire is characterised fundamentally by a lack of boundaries: Empire's rule has no limits' (p. xv). They outlined two key things we must keep in mind if we are to understand the concept of empire, and for them, both of these things are predicated on the boundless nature of empire.

Firstly, they say that, predicated on the boundless nature of empire, 'the concept of Empire posits a regime that effectively encompasses the spatial totality, or really that rules over the entre "civilised" world. No territorial boundaries limit its reign' (Hardt & Negri, 2000, p. xv). Secondly, they say that, again predicated on the boundless nature of empire, 'the concept of the Empire presents itself not as a historical regime originating in conquest, but rather as an order that effectively suspends history and thereby fixes the existing state of affairs for eternity' (Hardt & Negri, 2000, p. xv). In view of the aforementioned statements, they say that

> the Empire we are faced with wields enormous powers of oppression and destruction, but the fact should not make us nostalgic in any way

> for old forms of domination. The passage to Empire and its globalization offer new possibilities to forces of liberation.
>
> (Hardt & Negri, 2000, p. xv)

The intersection between Empire 1.0 and Empire 2.0 was not and is not only a theoretical concern for decolonial academics, it was and is also a practical concern for decolonial politicians and policy makers. For instance, at the famous Bandung Conference which gave birth to the Non-Aligned Movement, President Sukarno of Indonesia said:

> I beg of you do not think of colonialism only in the classical form which we of Indonesia, and our brothers in different parts of Asia and Africa, knew. Colonialism has its modern dress, in the form of economic control, intellectual control, actual physical control by a small but alien community within the nation. It is a skillful and determined enemy, and it appears in many disguises. It does not give up its loot easily.
>
> (qtd. in The Ministry of Foreign Affairs, 1955, p. 23)

Sukarno's speech was aimed at awakening the would-be members of the Non-Aligned Movement (the Third World) to the transformation or metamorphosis of imperialism, both the First World or Western imperialism and the Second World or Eastern imperialism. Basically, he wanted the non-aligned states to be aware and conscious of the fact that imperialism was still existing even though it has changed.

It will not be far-fetched to say that Sukarno needed to warn non-aligned states that imperialism was still existing even though it has changed because many people were used to the traditional conceptualisations of imperialism and empire and could only recognise Empire 1.0. Many people were not conscious that change has happened or was happening. Talking about leaders of non-aligned states needing Sukarno's warning, we must remember that these leaders themselves gathered to form the Non-Aligned Movement because they were conscious of the fact that change has happened or is happening as far as both the idea and practice of empire were concerned. For instance, there were even non-aligned leaders who were not conscious of such changes, with notable exceptions including the likes of Josip Broz Tito, Jawaharlal Nehru, Gamal Abdel Nasser and Kwame Nkrumah (1965) who himself expended a lot of time, space and resources, both intellectual and political, on fighting neocolonialism.

From Tito, to Nehru, Nasser, Sukarno and Nkrumah, we see political leaders who understood the shift from Empire 1.0 to Empire 2.0 and consequently understood that the hitherto conceptions of imperialism and empire may no longer be fit for purpose. As Muldoon (1999) says two and half decades ago, hitherto, the discourse on

> the concepts of empire and emperor has dealt with political units and political actors who occupied real political space. The concept of empire involved actual governments and officials or, at the very least, as in papal political theory, individuals who carried out real governmental functions under papal supervision.
>
> (p. 101)

But having understood the shift from Empire 1.0 to Empire 2.0, political leaders such as Tito, Nehru, Nasser, Sukarno and Nkrumah, among others, through a concerted effort, mounted a spirited political campaign to awaken the Third World to the realisation that the hitherto conceptualisations of imperialism and empire needed updating.

Even though we are accustomed to dealing with the concept of empire and many people accept that the phenomenon I referred to as Empire 1.0 actually existed, we are not used to dealing with the concept of metaphysical empire, and many people do not accept that the phenomenon I referred to as Empire 2.0 exists. Nevertheless, as you can see from the aforementioned discussion, even though many people are not used to the concept of metaphysical empire and even though many people do not agree that Empire 2.0 exists, the concept of metaphysical empire is not a misnomer because, according to Muldoon (1999),

> empire and emperor could have other meanings, however, meanings that were metaphysical or mystical or moral, not identifying real people and institutions but providing an explanation of God's providential plan for mankind or judging a form of government that morally corrupted those who practiced it.
>
> (p. 101)

Muldoon's explanation demonstrates the complexity of the concept of empire. Part of the complexity of the concept of empire is that it could mean different things to different people who lived in different places and who lived at different times. If we trace the history of imperialism and empire from medieval times to modern or contemporary times, we will see that the concept of empire actually meant different things at different times. Again, as Muldoon (1999) says two and half decades ago, the metaphysical conceptualisation of:

> empire and emperor had a long history, originating long before the Middle Ages. As the earlier discussion of Dante's *De Monarchia* pointed out, the concept of empire could refer to a divinely ordained sequence of great powers, four world monarchies or empires, engaged in a conflict that would eventually lead to a single great empire. The wars and struggles that characterised the history of the Near East and the Mediterranean world, the known world of the ancient and early

> medieval eras, could be reduced to a teleological schema that ultimately led to the fullness of God's plan. In other words, the concept of empire could have a metaphysical reality, describing an institution that played a unique role in the providential plan for mankind. In such a perspective, the actual empires were of little significance in themselves, acquiring their importance from their role in the divine plan.
>
> (p. 101)

It may not be contentious to argue that the concept of metaphysical empire is gaining traction in the decolonisation debate, and consequently, the concept may soon be *en vogue* in the debate. It may even be less contentious to argue that the concept is an accurate description of the phenomenon or condition it is intended to describe. Nevertheless, it is more contentious to say that it is largely or widely accepted that the phenomenon or condition the concept is intended to describe is a danger or threatening or at least undesirable or unacceptable phenomenon or condition.

To understand the concept of the metaphysical empire, the phenomenon or condition it is intended to describe, whether the description is accurate or not, and whether the phenomenon or condition should be seen as a danger or threatening, or at least undesirable or unacceptable phenomenon or condition, one needs to first understand the concept of colonialism. Colonialism is essentially 'a practice that involves both the subjugation of one people to another and the political and economic control of a dependent territory (or parts of it)' (Ypi, 2013, p. 162). It is 'a particular model of political organisation, typified by settler and exploitation colonies, and is best seen as one specific instance of imperialism, understood as the domination of a territory by a separate metropole' (Butt, 2013, p. 892).

Daniel Butt (2013) says colonialism essentially involves three ways of domination. Firstly, the coloniser denies the colonised self-determination, and the former imposes 'rule rooted in a separate political jurisdiction' on the latter (p. 893). Secondly, the coloniser attempts to impose its 'culture and customs onto the colonised, whether as a result of a belief in the racial and/or cultural superiority of the colonising power … or as a mechanism for establishing and consolidating political control' (Butt, 2013, p. 893). Thirdly, the coloniser exploits the colonised (Butt, 2013, p. 893).

In contradistinction to colonialism which involves the aforementioned three ways of domination, the metaphysical empire involves only the aforementioned second way of domination. In this sense, the metaphysical empire simultaneously involves: (1) a former metropolis' attempt to impose its culture and customs onto a former empire, 'whether as a result of a belief in the racial and/or cultural superiority' of the metropolis, 'or as a mechanism for establishing and consolidating political control' (Butt, 2013, p. 893); and (2) the acceptance of, or at least acquiescence to, the imposition in (1) by the empire.

In contrast with the tangible physical geographical empire, Ngugi Wa Thiong'o (2013, 2014) posits that there exists an intangible non-physical and non-geographical metaphysical empire. Corroborating Wa Thiong'o's thesis, Sabelo J. Ndlovu-Gatsheni (2018) explains that:

> the metaphysical empire co-exists with the commercial- non-territorial-military empire with its insatiable appetite for strategic economic resources. The metaphysical empire operates and subsists on invasion of the mental universe of the world. Consequently, it unleashes epistemicides, linguicides and cultural imperialism. Mental dislocation cascades from the invasion of the mental universe. The introduction of imperial languages and the displacement of indigenous languages were deliberate interventions of the metaphysical empire on colonised spaces. Inevitably, it provoked epistemological decolonisation, which is predicated on the demands for cognitive justice as an essential pre-requisite for re-humanisation/re-membering of the dehumanised and dismembered.
>
> (p. 96)

Wa Thiong'o (1993) is particularly concerned about mental control as a critical aspect of the metaphysical empire, and consequently metal emancipation as a critical aspect of decolonisation. From Marcus Mosiah Garvey to Robert Nesta Marley (Bob Marley), both mental slavery and the emancipation from mental slavery are recurrent themes in Black liberation struggles and the life-world of the Black person. So, Wa Thiong'o is in good company.

Like Garvey and Marley, Wa Thiong'o (1997) thinks that 'mind control through culture was the key! Cultural subjugation was a necessary condition for economic and political mastery' (pp. 8–9). Consequently, according to Ndlovu-Gatsheni (2018), in the twenty-first century, decoloniality or the decolonial project entails a decolonisation that is targeted at the 'metaphysical empire,' compared to the decolonisation of the twentieth century that targeted the 'physical empire' (Ndlovu-Gatsheni, 2018).

In spite of Wa Thiong'o's and Ndlovu-Gatsheni's concerns about the danger of the metaphysical empire and in spite of their clamour for a decolonisation that is targeted at the metaphysical empire, there is no canonical agreement or consensus on the danger of the metaphysical empire and the need for the decolonisation of the metaphysical empire. As already mentioned, even the existence of the metaphysical empire has been questioned – not everyone agrees that the metaphysical empire exists.

Cultural appropriationists such as Chinua Achebe, Wole Soyinka and Chimamanda Adichie think that we can appropriate colonial heritage such as the English language and use it as if it were part and parcel of the African culture, and that this is in no way antithetical to decolonisation. But mutual exclusivists such as Wa Thiong'o and Ndlovu-Gatsheni argue that authentic decolonisation entails that we must completely dissociate the African and her culture from colonial heritage.

Whether consciously or unconsciously, *prima facie*, the mutual exclusivism argument is predicated on the belief or fear that appropriating a European colonial language is tantamount to acquiescing to African and Black racial inferiority and European and White racial superiority. For mutual exclusivists, such acquiescence is essentially an acquiescence to the negation of (Black) African identity. So, the concept of identity (and the concept of racial identity) plays a key role in the metaphysical empire debate.

The mutual exclusivists' belief or fear is not necessarily delusional because 'it is well known that the race concept has been used to justify gross forms of injustice: slavery, genocide, colonial subjugation and exploitation, forced segregation and arbitrary civic exclusion, and land and resource expropriation' (Shelby, 2012, p. 337). So, for mutual exclusivists, *plus ca change, plus c'est la meme chose* – the more things change, the more they remain the same. Consequently, the onus is on cultural appropriationists to prove that 'this time is different'.

The disagreement between mutual exclusivists and cultural appropriationists creates a dilemma in the decolonisation debate; to decolonise or not to decolonise, that is the question. In view of this dilemma, in this book, on the one hand, I shall test the validity of mutual exclusivism. On the other hand, I shall explore the strengths and weaknesses of cultural appropriationism. So, in this book, in an original, novel and seminal way, I shall reconcile mutual exclusivism and appropriationism by creating an intermediary position between these two extremes on the metaphysical empire debate.

Ultimately, in the discussion of this book, I shall demonstrate that what the dilemma of decolonisation entails is that even in the face of the danger of the metaphysical empire, the decolonisation project can still be accommodative. An accommodative decolonisation, recognising the relationship between cultural universals and cultural particulars, creates room for cultural appropriation because it sees certain things as human achievement rather than African, European, American, Asian, Arabic or Chinese achievement.

The Scope and Content of the Metaphysical Empire

Discussing the scope and content of the metaphysical empire is a good starting point to demonstrate that what the dilemma of the decolonisation entails even in the face of the danger of the metaphysical empire is that the decolonisation project can still be accommodative. Such discussion is not tantamount to the aforementioned demonstration. Nevertheless, it lays the foundation for such demonstration.

To understand the scope and content of the metaphysical empire, we need to take another look at mutual exclusivists' perception of, and reaction to, the appropriation of European languages. Looking at how mutual exclusivists react to the appropriation of European languages and perceive such linguistic appropriation, the importance of perception cannot be over-emphasised because of three reasons. Firstly, empire, whether physical or metaphysical, is essentially a power relations game. In every form of power relations, perception matters, and it matters a lot.

Second, perception is even more important in view of, to reiterate, the historical fact that 'the race concept has been used to justify gross forms of injustice: slavery, genocide, colonial subjugation and exploitation, forced segregation and arbitrary civic exclusion, and land and resource expropriation' (Shelby, 2012, p. 337).

Thirdly, perception matters because, although 'the literature on attitude change … illuminate[s] the ways that discrepant information does in fact alter established views,' consequently, no one should be left with 'the impression that beliefs and images never change'; nevertheless, 'images of others, once established, are hard to dislodge' (Jervis, 2017, p. 10). It seems while images of Europeans might have changed for cultural appropriationists, they have not changed for mutual exclusivists.

The aforementioned perception and reaction to the appropriation of European colonial languages, from a mutual exclusivist perspective, are justifiable because, as Wa Thiong'o (2017) reminds us, in every case of European 'colonial conquest, language was meant to complete what the sword had started: do to the mind what the sword had done to the body' (s.p.). As he succinctly puts it, 'the bullet was the means of the physical subjugation. Language was the means of the spiritual subjugation' (Wa Thiong'o qtd. in wa Ngugi, 2018, s.p.).

The veracity of Wa Thiong'o's claim should not be in doubt if one looks at the history of European colonialism. For instance:

> in 19th century Indian … in the famous minutes on Indian education in 1934, Macaulay advocated English as a medium of education in India in order to create a class of people Indian in blood and colour but otherwise English in mentality and everything else. The same was happening in those spheres under the other European powers. The French and Portuguese called their version of the Macaulayean process assimilation. Language was the key factor in assimilation. But neither the French, the Portuguese nor the British went through this exercise for the aesthetics of assimilation. As Macaulay put it bluntly, it was to create linguistically Westernised middlemen who would automatically carry out the intent of the ruler on the masses of the ruled.
>
> (Wa Thiong'o qtd. in wa Ngugi, 2018, s.p.).

Whether it is Great Britain, France, Belgium, Portugal, Spain, Germany, the Netherlands or Italy, every European coloniser imposed or at least tried to impose its language on its colonies. In the case of Great Britain, one can even trace the linguistic strategy back to the eighteenth century even before the imposition of English on its African and Asian colonies. A careful observation of the history of the British empire will reveal to any observer that

> even the 18th century struggles for the standardisation of English had both a national and an imperial intent: A Standardised English would become the building block of … a metaphysical empire, an empire of language and literature that would outlive the actual physical British empire.
>
> (Wa Thiong'o, 2017, s.p.; see Beach, 2001)

For the aforementioned reasons, Wa Thiong'o (2017) argues that the situation of Africa's continuous dependence on European languages

> is not the consequence of an accident of history: it is the fulfilment of a conscious imperial design in a long history of conquest …. Among these is a power relationship between the language of the conqueror and the language of the vanquished.
>
> (s.p.)

In essence, Wa Thiong'o (2017)'s argument is that:

> along with the economic and political empires, Europe simultaneously and consciously created empires of the mind through language ideologies and practices, empires in tune with their world view and practical needs. They gave us their accents in exchange for their access to our resources. … Europe gave Africa the resources of their accent; Africa gave Europe access to the resources of the continent. So when African intellectuals and leaders were busy protecting their borrowed accents, Europe and the West were busy sharpening their instruments for access to the resources of the continent. Accents for Access … That, unfortunately, is the story of post-colonial Africa.
>
> (s.p.)

In Empire 1.0 the focus of the decolonial project is on political and economic liberation, while in Empire 2.0 the focus of the decolonial project is on cultural (in general) and linguistic (in particular) liberation. Most decolonialists are more concerned about Empire 1.0 and less concerned about Empire 2.0. But Wa Thiong'o (1986) thinks that we should focus more on Empire 2.0 because, in his view, in the struggle for liberation, what he refers to as the cultural bomb is 'the biggest weapon wielded and actually daily unleashed by imperialism against the collective defiance waged by the colonised against the colonisers' (p. 3).

One may or may not agree with Wa Thiong'o that cultural imperialism is more pernicious than political and economic imperialism. One may think that, in comparison with the impact of political and economic imperialism, he was exaggerating the impact of cultural imperialism. Nevertheless, one cannot plausibly deny that his fundamental claim about cultural imperialism is historical and factual. In his description or explanation of cultural imperialism, he says that:

> The effect of the cultural bomb is to annihilate a people's belief in their names, in their language, in their environment, in their heritage of struggle, in their unity, in their capacities and ultimately in themselves. It makes them see their past as one wasteland of non-achievement and it makes them want to distance themselves from that wasteland. It makes them want to identify with that which is furthest removed from themselves; for instance, with other people's languages rather than their own. It makes them identify with that which is decadent and reactionary, all those forces which would stop their own springs of life. It even plants serious doubts about the moral rightness of struggle. Possibilities of triumph or victory are seen as remote, ridiculous dreams. The intended results are despair, despondency, and a collective death-wish. Amidst this wasteland which it has created, imperialism presents itself as the cure and demands that the dependent sing hymns of praise with the constant refrain: 'Theft is holy.'
>
> (Wa Thiong'o, 1986, p. 3) (emphasis in original)

Regardless of whether Wa Thiong'o is right or wrong that cultural imperialism is more pernicious than political imperialism, both the former and the latter are cut from the same cloth. Just as Wa Thiong'o thinks that cultural imperialism is pervasive, so too I think that global social, political and economic inequality and injustice pervades the contemporary world. After all, it is evident that our world is characterised by global inequality and injustice.

It may not be contentious to assert that such inequality and injustice characterise Global North-Global South relations both at the institutional level (rules, norms and practices that shape and regulate the relationship between the former or its members, states and organisations and the latter or its members, states and organisations) and the interactional level (between the citizens of the former and the citizens of the latter). It may even be less contentious to assert that it is a *fait accompli* that such interactional and institutional inequality and injustice especially affect African states and citizens. In other words, since Africa is the poorest region in the world, since African states are the poorest states in the world, and since Africans are the poorest people in the world, Africa is the region usually and always, or at least mostly, at the receiving end of such interactional and institutional inequality and injustice.

Basically, the pattern of the division of the advantages and disadvantages that are generated by global economic and political interaction and cooperation or competition is skewed in favour of the globally well-off and to the detriment of the globally worse-off. The well-off is the Global North, while the worse-off is the Global South. Since Africa is the poorest region in the Global South, Africa and Africans are the most globally economically and politically disadvantaged region and people in the world. For this reason, cultural appropriationists, like mutual exclusivists, should be worried about global inequality and injustice, and such global inequality and injustice should prompt both cultural appropriationists and mutual exclusivists to revisit their positions vis-à-vis the decolonisation project.

The pattern that the aforementioned global inequality and injustice follows is in some ways similar to the pattern that cultural imperialism follows. In other words, what makes political and economic imperialism successful is in some ways similar to what makes cultural imperialism successful. In political and economic imperialism, the patterns of political and economic power relations are designed to advantage the perpetrators of imperialism and disadvantage the victims. Similarly, in cultural imperialism, the patterns of cultural power relations are designed to favour the imperialists and disfavour the so-called natives.

It is in view of this situation that Wa Thiong'o thinks that cultural imperialism and political and economic imperialism go *pari passu* even though he thinks that cultural imperialism is more pernicious than political and economic imperialism. Again, whether he is right or wrong that cultural imperialism is more pernicious than political and economic imperialism, there is no doubt that he is right that the metaphysical empire, at least in the aspect of language, has been very potent. As Ndlovu-Gatsheni (2018) argues,

> the success of the 'metaphysical empire' has been in its submission of the colonised world to European memory. The consequence has been the re-making of the African people in the image of the colonial conqueror. Metaphysical empire even invented new political identities such as 'native.'
>
> (p. 100) (emphasis in original)

The success of cultural imperialism (in general) and the adoption of European colonial languages (in particular) by Africans are especially worrisome for Wa Thiong'o because, in his view, 'language carries, and culture carries, particularly through orature and literature, the entire bodies of values by which we come to perceive ourselves and our place in the world' (qtd. in wa Ngugi, 2018, s.p.).

For him, the adoption of European colonial languages by Africans is tantamount of having a death-wish for African languages. As he says:

> The explanation of the death-wish for one's own language and the embrace of the dominant other has to go beyond the uses or not of the languages in question. It probably lies in how that sense of dominance was brought about. A common thread in export of English in … Africa was the constant association of extreme humiliation and negativity with native languages and the corresponding value and prestige associated with English in colonial education factories …. One set of languages was associated with defeat, shame, incoherence, savagery even, and the other with modernity, science, conquest and being human. No wonder people would want to bask in the sunshine of the language of glory and hide from those of shame and defeat.
>
> (Wa Thiong'o, 2017, s.p.)

As far as wa Thiong'o is concerned, to adopt European colonial languages is to engage in cultural and linguistic self-destruction irrespective of the nominal and ephemeral gains such adoption might appear to provide. For instance, he says that by adopting European languages, 'African scholarship has achieved … great visibility in the world by the tremendous feat of making itself invisible to Africa' (Wa Thiong'o, 2017, s.p.).

> For him, by adopting European languages, 'African scholarship wears a linguistic mask with the magic quality of making it invisible to the majority in Africa and simultaneously visible to those with the key made in Europe'
>
> (Wa Thiong'o, 2017, s.p.)

Consequently, in spite of the aforementioned great visibility of African scholarship, and because of the linguistic mask, by adopting European languages, 'we can only see ourselves through European eyes, at the minimum. This makes us look at Africa with the eyes of an outsider, thus in effect giving up on our responsibility to secure the continent for African people' (Wa Thiong'o, 2017, s.p.).

For Wa Thiong'o, what is happening here, essentially, is that African scholars, through their adoption of European languages, identify with Europeans but alienate fellow Africans. Because of such identification, they vicariously live, think and act as Europeans, albeit pseudo-Europeans in a mimetic way. But because of such alienation, they are, on behalf of Europeans, destroying their own African culture and language.

In 1986, recollecting his participation in the 1962 African Writers of English Expression conference, Wa Thiong'o (1986) says:

> Now looking back from the self-questioning heights of 1986, I can see this contained absurd anomalies. I, a student, could qualify for the meeting on the basis of only two published short stories …. But

> neither Shaban Robert, then the greatest living East African poet with several works of poetry and prose to his credit in Kiswahili, nor Chief Fagunwa, the great writer with several published titles in Yoruba, could possibly qualify.
>
> (qtd. in wa Ngugi, 2018, s.p.)

Wa Thiong'o (2017) follows in the footsteps of Nkrumah for whom 'African languages were central in African scholarship, development and the [continent's] relationship to the diaspora and the world' (s.p.). Like Nkrumah, Wa Thiong'o is not calling 'for linguistic self-isolation for he saw the role of other languages like Arabic, English, French and Portuguese' (Wa Thiong'o, 2017, s.p.).

But like Nkrumah, he evidently thinks that African languages are not, and should not be, 'a lower rung on the ladder to an English heaven but rather as equal partners in the construction of a common but multilingual heaven' (Wa Thiong'o, 2017, s.p.).

In his own summary of his position, he says that his defence of African languages against the adoption of European colonial languages 'does not mean and should never mean retreating into linguistic self-isolation' (Wa Thiong'o, 2017, s.p.)
Rather, the point he is making is that

> if you know all the languages of the world and you do not know your mother tongue or the language of your culture, that is enslavement. But if you know your mother tongue or the language of your culture, and add all the other languages of the world to it, that is empowerment.
>
> (Wa Thiong'o, 2017, s.p.)

In view of the aforementioned claim, when presented with the option of enslavement and the option of empowerment as described, Wa Thiong'o (2017) says it is a no-brainer that Africans will want the latter rather than the former. He says Africans certainly want an Africa that is 'economically, politically, culturally and psychologically empowered, an Africa secure in its base, even as it engages with other peoples and continents' (s.p.).

The Structure of the Book

In the penultimate and preceding sub-chapters, I explained what the metaphysical empire is, and what its scope and content are. In a novel way, in the aforementioned sub-chapters, I juxtaposed the physical empire with the metaphysical empire, extended the domain of the metaphysical empire beyond its usual linguistic domain, and preliminarily explored the place of the metaphysical empire in the decolonisation project and the extent to which the project should or should not be concerned with the metaphysical empire.

Based on the preliminary exploration in this introductory chapter, in the next chapter (Chapter 2) I shall engage in an advanced exploration of the debate between cultural appropriationists and mutual exclusivists. The former think that we can appropriate colonial heritage such as the English language and use it as if it were part and parcel of the African culture, and that this is in no way antithetical to decolonisation. But the latter argue that authentic decolonisation entails that we must completely dissociate the African and her culture from colonial heritage.

The English, French, Portuguese, Spanish, German and Afrikaans (South African version of Dutch) languages in Africa are relics of colonialism, and as such, are residual colonialism. Being residual colonialism, for mutual exclusivists, these languages are part and parcel of the metaphysical empire. Consequently, in the post-colony, to hold on to these White and European languages which were used in the colony and not to return to the African languages of the pre-colony is to allow oneself to be subjected to the metaphysical empire and consent to be a subject of the metaphysical empire. In the chapter, I shall delve into the aforementioned debate by, on the one hand, exploring the strengths and weaknesses of cultural appropriationism and, on the other hand, testing the validity of mutual exclusivism.

Following my discussion in this introductory chapter and in Chapter 2 – having explained what the metaphysical empire is in this introductory chapter, and having resolved the quandary between cultural appropriationism and mutual exclusivism in Chapter 2 – in Chapter 3 I shall explain the key role of the concept of identity (and the concept of racial identity) in the metaphysical empire debate.

In Chapter 4, taking a cue from Kwasi Wiredu (1995, 1997), I shall draw insights from metaphysics to simultaneously delineate the (metaphorical) boundaries of the metaphysical empire and tease out the grounds on which African cultures can appropriate some useful aspects of Western cultures without the danger of falling into the metaphysical empire. As we shall see in the chapter:

> Arguably, Wiredu's particular contribution to the debate on the origins, status, problematic and future of contemporary African philosophy resides in his formulations regarding his theory of conceptual decolonisation. His approach in formulating this theory of discursive agency and more specifically philosophical practice involves the incorporation of a form of bi-culturalism. In other words, his approach entails analyses of

> the canon of Western philosophy and also the manifestations of [... African] cultures as a way of attaining a conceptual synthesis.
>
> (Osha, n.d., sect. 6)

Like Wiredu (1997), I shall 'confront the paradox that while Western cultures recoil from claims of universality, previously colonised peoples, seeking to redefine their identities, insist on cultural particularities' (s.p.).[1] Like Wiredu (1997), I think that 'universals, rightly conceived on the basis of our common biological identity, are not incompatible with cultural particularities and, in fact, are what make intercultural communication possible' (s.p.).[2]

My discussion on cultural universals and cultural particulars in Chapter 4 demonstrates that cultural appropriation without the danger of falling into the metaphysical empire is possible. But this poses a problem for the decolonisation project, namely where does decolonisation begin and end or where should the project start and stop. In view of this dilemma, in Chapter 5 I shall explore different pertinent issues such as: theoretical plausibility versus practicable possibility (what may be possible in theory but not in practice in the decolonisation project?); theoretical imperative versus practical necessity (what does decolonisation require both in theory and in practice vis-à-vis the metaphysical empire?); and the authenticity argument (that is, returning to and retaining original African language) versus the efficiency argument (that is, easier to appropriate and use Western languages).

What the dilemma of decolonisation suggests is that even in the face of the danger of the metaphysical empire, the decolonisation project can still be accommodative. An accommodative decolonisation, recognising the relationship between cultural universals and particulars, simultaneously promotes the originality and authenticity of African cultures and creates room for cultural appropriation because it sees certain things as human achievement rather than African, European, American, Asian, Arabic or Chinese achievement.

In view of the discussion in this introductory chapter, and from Chapters 2 to 5, in the concluding chapter I shall argue that both cultural appropriationists and mutual exclusivists must simultaneously renounce absolutism (this does not mean they should embrace relativism) and be amenable to fusion of horizons. Consequently, I shall propose fusion of horizons as the way forward for the discourse on the metaphysical empire.

In the concluding chapter, taking a cue from Hans-Georg Gadamer (1989), firstly I shall begin by concurring that it is important to have a horizon because 'a person who has no horizon does not see far enough and hence overvalues what is nearest to him' (p. 302). In his words, 'every finite present has its limitations. We define the concept of "situation" by saying that it represents a standpoint that limits the possibility of vision. Hence essential to the concept of a situation is the concept of a "horizon"' (p. 302) (emphasis in original).

Therefore, importantly, one must fuse his or her horizon with the horizons of others in order for one to go beyond the limits of his or her own horizon. Fusing one's horizon with the horizons of others means that one is able to change standpoints and step out of one's own horizon, and 'the merely changing of standpoints entails the possibility of having different horizons and the mere stepping out of our horizons entails the possibility of having broader horizons' (Abumere, 2015, p. 36).

Secondly, I shall continue by clarifying that

> fusion of horizons is not Hegelian dialectics of, say, being + nothingness = becoming, or thesis + antithesis = synthesis which itself becomes a new thesis. Nevertheless, fusion of horizons occurs when individuals understand that the context of their discourse can be seen from a different perspective in order to reach a new conclusion.
>
> (Abumere, 2015, p. 193; see Vessey, n.d., s.p.)

Finally, I shall explain that by arguing that both cultural appropriationists and mutual exclusivists must simultaneously renounce absolutism (this does not mean they should embrace relativism) and be amenable to fusion of horizons, and by proposing fusion of horizons as the way forward for the discourse on the metaphysical empire, I avoid what I refer to as the decolonisation fallacy which is tantamount to arguing that things are always either/or. Things are not always either/or. Things are either/or if the options are A and non-A; that is if one is necessarily correct, the other being the logical opposite must be necessarily wrong. But if the options are A, B, they can be neither/nor if both are wrong, but it can also be A and B if both are right. Furthermore, either of them can be fully or partially right or wrong. So things can also be partially A and partially B, partially A and fully B, or fully A and partially B (Abumere, 2015).

Notes

1 See the description on the cover page of *Cultural Universals and Particulars: An African Perspective*. See Bibliography for full details.
2 See the description on the cover page of *Cultural Universals and Particulars: An African Perspective*. See Bibliography for full details.

Bibliography

Abumere, F. A. (2015) *Different Perspectives on Global Justice: A Fusion of Horizons*. Bielefeld, Publication at Bielefeld University (PUB).

Beach, A. R. (2001) The creation of a classical language in the eighteenth century: Standardising English, cultural imperialism, and the future of the literary canon. *Texas Studies in Literature and Language* 43 (2), 117–141.

Boron, A. B. (2005) *Empire and Imperialism: A Critical Reading of Michael Hardt and Antonio Negri*. London, Zed Books.

Butt, D. (2013) Colonialism and postcolonialism. In: LaFollette, H. (ed.) *The International Encyclopedia of Ethics*, 2nd ed., s.p. Hoboken, New Jersey, Wiley and Sons.

Gadamer, H.-G. (1989) *Truth and Method*. New York, Crossroad.

Hardt, M., & Negri, A. (2000). *Empire*. Cambridge, MA, Harvard University Press.

Jervis, R. (2017) *Perception and Misperception in International Politics*, rev. ed. Princeton, NJ, Princeton University Press.

Muldoon, J. (1999) *Empire and Order: The Concept of Empire, 800–1800*. London, Palgrave Macmillan.

Ndlovu-Gatsheni, S. J. (2018) Metaphysical empire, linguicides and cultural imperialism. *English Academy Review* 35 (2), 96–115.

Nkrumah, K. (1965) *Neo-colonialism*. London, Thomas Nelson.

Osha, S. (n.d.) Kwasi Wiredu (1931–2022). *Internet Encyclopedia of Philosophy*. https://iep.utm.edu/wiredu/ Accessed: July 10, 2024.

Shelby, T. (2012) Race. In: Estlund, D. (ed.) *The Oxford Handbook of Political Philosophy*. Oxford, Oxford University Press, pp. 336–353.

The Ministry of Foreign Affairs (1955) *Asia-Africa speaks from Bandung*. The Ministry of Foreign Affairs, Jakarta, Republic of Indonesia.

Vessey, D. (n.d.) Gadamer and the fusion of horizons. www.davevessey.com/gadamer_Horizons.htm

Wa Ngugi, M. (2018) What decolonising the mind means today. Literary Hub, March 23. https://worldpece.org/sites/default/files/artifacts/media/pdf/mukoma_wa_ngugi-_what_decolonizing_the_mind_means_today_literary_hub.pdf

Wa Thiong'o, N. (1986) *Decolonising the Mind: The Politics of Language in African Literature*. Oxford, James Currey.

Wa Thiong'o, N. (1993) *Moving the Centre: The Struggle for Cultural Freedoms*. Oxford, James Currey.

Wa Thiong'o, N. (1997) *Writers in Politics: A Re-Engagement with Issues of Literature and Society*. Oxford, James Currey.

Wa Thiong'o, N. (2013). Resisting metaphysical empires: Language as a war zone.' The Third John La Rose Memorial Lecture, Senate House, University of London, London, October 2.

Wa Thiong'o, N. (2014) *Resisting Metaphysical Empires: Language as a War Zone*. London, New Beacon Books.

Wa Thiong'o, N. (2017) African languages – lifting the mask of invisibility. *University World News*. Mach 10. https://www.universityworldnews.com/post.php?story=20170307102246629

Wiredu, K. (1995) The concept of mind with particular references to the language and thought of the Akan. In: Kwame, S. (ed.) *Readings in African Philosophy: An Akan Collection*. Lanham, MD, University Press of America, pp. 120–136.

Wiredu, K. (1997) *Cultural Universals and Particulars: An African Perspective*. Bloomington, IN, Indiana University Press.

Ypi, L. (2013) What's wrong with colonialism. *Philosophy and Public Affairs* 41 (2), 158–191.

2 Cultural Appropriationism versus Mutual Exclusivism

Concepts and Conceptualisations Matter, and They Matter Seriously

Based on the preliminary exploration in the preceding chapter, in this chapter I shall engage in an advanced exploration of the debate between cultural appropriationists and mutual exclusivists. In this chapter, I shall delve into the aforementioned debate by, on the one hand, exploring the strengths and weaknesses of cultural appropriationism and, on the other hand, testing the validity of mutual exclusivism.

In the metaphysical empire debate, remember that cultural appropriationists such as Chinua Achebe (1988), Wole Soyinka and Chimamanda Ngozi Adichie think that we can appropriate colonial heritage such as the English language and use it as if it were part and parcel of the African culture, and that this is in no way antithetical to decolonisation. But mutual exclusivists such as Ngugi Wa Thiong'o (1986, 1993, 1997, 2009a, 2009b, 2012, 2014, 2016, 2017; see wa Ngugi, 2018) and Sabelo J. Ndlovu-Gatsheni (2013a, 2013b, 2016, 2018a, 2018b, 2019, see Ndlovu-Gatsheni & Zondi, 2016) argue that authentic decolonisation entails that we must completely dissociate the African and her culture from colonial heritage.

In the metaphysical empire debate, we are presented with only two options, namely cultural appropriationism and mutual exclusivism, and are asked to choose either the former or the latter. The problem with being restricted to choosing either cultural appropriationism or mutual exclusivism is that both of these positions are extremes. On a spectrum, mutual exclusivism is at the 0 end of the spectrum and cultural appropriationism is at the 1 end of the spectrum.

Anything from 0.1 to 0.9 on the spectrum is discounted by the aforementioned 'extremism.' Nevertheless, on the one hand, since 0.1 to 0.4 tilt towards mutual exclusivism, mutual exclusivists might be a little bit tolerant of 0.1 to 0.4 even though they will not be readily receptive of it. So too since 0.6 to 0.9 tilt towards cultural appropriationism, cultural appropriationists might be a little bit tolerant of 0.6 to 0.9 even though they will not

DOI: 10.4324/9781003589839-2

be readily receptive of it. On the other hand, since 0.6 to 0.9 tilts towards cultural appropriationism, mutual exclusivists will readily discount it. So too since 0.1 to 0.4 tilts towards mutual exclusivism, cultural appropriationists will readily discount it.

On the spectrum, 0.5 sits perfectly at the middle of the road between the 0 extreme end of mutual exclusivism and the 1 extreme end of cultural appropriationism. I think this middle of the road position should be an option in the metaphysical empire debate. We may or may not be able to have an approach that will sit perfectly in the 0.5 position. But any position such as 0.4 or 0.6 that can approximate to 0.5 works just as well as 0.5. This is what I aim to achieve with accommodative decolonisation, qualified decolonisation or decolonisation with a caveat – I will return to the matter of accommodative decolonisation in the fifth and concluding chapters.

In the metaphysical empire debate, to present mutual exclusivism and cultural appropriationism as the only options and restrict us to choosing either the former or the latter is tantamount to arguing that things are always either/or. Things are not always either/or. Things are either/or if the options are A and non-A; that is if one is necessarily correct, the other being the logical opposite must be necessarily wrong. But if the options are A, B, they can be neither/nor if both are wrong, but it can also be A and B if both are right. Furthermore, either of them can be fully or partially right or wrong. So things can also be partially A and partially B, partially A and fully B, or fully A and partially B (Abumere, 2015).

In spite of my opposition to the extremes of mutual exclusivism and cultural appropriationism, I am simultaneously sympathetic to the former's wariness of cultural imperialism and the latter's attempt to transcend the fixation on colonialism and its derivatives. I think that anyone who attempts to transcend the fixation on colonialism and its derivatives must take into consideration the fact that such fixation does not happen in vacuum. It happens in the context of domination and the attempt to be free from the domination.

When mutual exclusivists complain about domination and when they are afraid that ceding cultural grounds to Europeans is an open invitation to be dominated, their complaint and fear are justified by history. Colonialism and its derivatives are not empty concepts; the denotations and connotations of these concepts are sufficient grounds for mutual exclusivists to be wary of any form of relationship – whether political, economic or cultural – between Africans and Europeans.

For this reason, I think that concepts and conceptualisations matter, and they matter seriously. It is when we take the concepts and conceptualisations of colonialism and its derivatives seriously that we are able to step into the shoes of mutual exclusivists and feel their fear, hear their complain and be sympathetic to their attempt at decolonisation even when we do not entirely agree with them, even when we only agree with them to a little extent, or even when we do not agree with them at all.

In view of the aforementioned reason, I think any juxtaposition of mutual exclusivism and cultural appropriationism that aims to be impartial will do well to begin with the clarification of concepts and terms. Such clarification must tell us what colonialism and its derivatives are or what they are perceived to be not by the coloniser who cannot be trusted to be impartial, and may be not even by the colonised who may be too emotional about the topic to remain purely analytic in her judgement, but by an impartial spectator who is both emotionally detached enough to remain purely analytic and trustworthy enough to be impartial.

So, beginning with the clarification of concepts and terms, we can see colonisation from the perspective of what Ndlovu-Gatsheni (2019) refers to as episodic school. In this sense, we can see colonisation as 'the event of conquest and rule over a conquered territory and a people, which was according to Jacob Ade Ajayi a "mere episode in African history"' (Ndlovu-Gatsheni, 2019, s.p.; see Ajayi, 1965; Ajayi, 1976) (emphasis in original). Then we can see colonialism from the perspective of what Ndlovu-Gatsheni (2019) refers to as epic school. In this sense, we can see colonialism as 'trans-historic power structure of colonial domination that survives dismantlement of administrative colonialism' (s.p.).

Combining the thoughts of Frantz Fanon (1968), Peter Ekeh (1975) and Ali Mazrui (1978, 1986) as Ndlovu-Gatsheni does, we can summarise colonialism as he does in the following succinct and apt ways. Colonialism, *a la* Fanon, re-engineers and manipulates the 'past of the oppressed people, and distorts, disfigures and destroys it' (qtd. in Ndlovu-Gatsheni, 2019, s.p.). Colonialism, *a la* Ekeh, represents a 'social movement of epochal dimensions whose enduring significance is beyond the life-span of the colonial situation' (Ndlovu-Gatsheni, 2019, s.p.). While *a la* Mazrui, colonialism represents 'a revolution of epic proportions' because 'what Africa knows about itself, what different parts of Africa know about each other, have been profoundly influenced by the West' (Ndlovu-Gatsheni, 2019, s.p.).

Taking a cue from Ndlovu-Gatsheni (2019), the concepts of coloniality, decolonisation and decoloniality can be understood in the following ways. He defines coloniality as the 'logic, culture, and structure of the modern world-system (colonialism and its replications)' (Ndlovu-Gatsheni, 2019). Then he defines decolonisation as the 'dismantlement of direct colonial administration and achievement of independence (shift of political power from colonial white ruling elite to black native elite: the struggle is that of elites who use peasants & workers as foot soldiers to gain state power)' (Ndlovu-Gatsheni, 2019). While he defines decoloniality as the 'new resurgent and insurgent movements confronting coloniality in the domains of power, being, and knowledge' (Ndlovu-Gatsheni, 2019).

In the same vein, taking a cue from Ndlovu-Gatsheni (2018a, 2018b, 2019) and adopting the ideas of Sampie Terreblanche (2014), Kwame Nkrumah (1964, 1965), Anibal Quijano (2000) and Ngugi Wa Thiong'o (1986, 1993, 1997, 2009a, 2009b, 2012, 2016), we can understand the place of the concept of empire and derivative concepts such as physical empire which requires political decolonisation, non-territorial commercial empire or neocolonialism, global coloniality which requires economic decolonisation, colonisation of the mind, and metaphysical empire itself in both the historical and contemporary affairs of Africa in the following ways.

Concerning empire, *a la* Terreblanche (2014),

> we cannot understand the challenges of our time without understanding the ways in which 500 years of Western empire building, often with the complicity of the elites of the Restern World, have shaped our world into the deeply unequal and gratuitously unjust place that it is today.
>
> (qtd. in Ndlovu-Gatsheni, 2019, s.p.)

Empire as a physical phenomenon, that is, physical empire, entailed the conquering and administration of 'the conquered people' and it requires political decolonisation (Ndlovu-Gatsheni, 2019, s.p.). It was for this reason that Nkrumah famously told Félix Houphouët-Boigny and others who wanted to seek economic development before political freedom to seek political independence first and economic independence will follow (Ndlovu-Gatsheni, 2019, s.p.).

Furthermore, on the one hand, empire as what Nkrumah (1965) refers to as neocolonialism or Ndlovu-Gatsheni (2019) refers to as non-territorial commercial empire 'remotely controls the world capitalist economy and has monopoly of weapons of mass destruction' (s.p.). Then global coloniality, *a la* Anibal Quijano (2000), represents 'struggles for New International Economic Order (NIEO)' and it requires economic decolonisation (Ndlovu-Gatsheni, 2019, s.p.).

On the other hand, metaphysical empire, *a la* Wa Thiong'o (1986, 1993, 1997, 2009a, 2009b, 2012, 2016), represents the 'invasion of the mental universe of the colonised and removal of the hard disk of previous African memory and knowledge and insertion of software of European memory and knowledge' (Ndlovu-Gatsheni, 2019, s.p.). While colonisation of the mind, *a la* Ndlovu-Gatsheni (2019), represents 'epistemicides, linguicides, culturecides, alienation and cultural imperialism: epistemological decolonisation' (s.p.). And for him, it requires 'epistemological decolonisation' (s.p.).

Looking at the aforementioned concepts or terms and their definitions, it is trite to mention that without colonialism, there will be no decolonisation. Even with colonialism, if colonialism were seen by all and sundry to be beneficial or benevolent, there will be no need for decolonisation. The clamour for decolonisation exists and subsists because colonialism is seen by many people in the Global South – and in the context of this book, Africa – to be an evil. To see colonialism as an evil is not to demonise colonialism or exaggerate its negative consequences. A mere cursory look, not even a thorough or careful one, at the concept, *raison d'être*, logic and *modus operandi* of colonialism suffices to see that it is indeed an evil.

Empire 2.0: Empires of the Mind

Just as without colonialism there will be no need for political and economic decolonisation, so too without cultural imperialism there will be no need for cultural decolonisation. If it is agreed that colonialism is evil, then, logically, one would expect that its derivative metaphysical empire must be evil too. However, as we have already seen and as I have already mentioned almost *ad nauseam*, the metaphysical empire is not generally accepted to be evil in spite of the fact that it is a derivative of colonialism; only mutual exclusivists see it as evil.

The fact that cultural appropriationists such as Achebe, Soyinka, Adichie and others who condemn political and economic imperialism do not condemn the metaphysical empire is worth pondering on. Apart from not condemning the metaphysical empire, the fact that they even go as far as accepting and promoting it is even more worth pondering on. When we ponder on their receptivity and promotion of cultural empire, what we are likely going to stumble on, or what we are certainly going to conclude, is that they simply understand the metaphysical empire differently from mutual exclusivists.

It is one thing to understand the metaphysical empire differently from mutual exclusivists. But it is another thing to see it as a positive phenomenon in spite of the fact that it is a derivative of the colonialism that the likes of Achebe, Soyinka and Adichie abhor. Could it be that they do not really understand what the metaphysical empire is? Could it be that in spite of their intellectual heights and expansive practical experiences they are still naïve about the intentions and never-ending scheming of Europeans to dominate Africans politically, economically and culturally? Could it be that the situation is none of the above? If so, could it be that mutual exclusivists exaggerate the derivativeness of the metaphysical empire from colonialism? Whatever the situation is, a concise and apt description of what exactly makes the metaphysical empire similar to or different from the physical empire will be very helpful.

To reiterate, the simplest way to understand the metaphysical empire is to understand it as Empire 2.0. This goes beyond merely saying what the metaphysical empire 'is.' It goes as far as adopting *via negativa* as a methodological device to say what the metaphysical empire 'is not.' This entails contrasting the tangible physical geographical empire with the intangible non-physical and non-geographical metaphysical empire. In this sense, while we see the tangible physical geographical empire as Empire 1.0, we see the intangible non-physical and non-geographical metaphysical empire as Empire 2.0.

In spite of Empire 2.0, cultural appropriationists think that we can appropriate colonial heritage such as the English language and use it as if it were part and parcel of the African culture, and that this is in no way antithetical to decolonization. But in view of Empire 2.0, mutual exclusivists argue that authentic decolonisation entails that we must completely dissociate the African and her culture from colonial heritage.

For mutual exclusivists, the English, French, Portuguese, Spanish, German and Afrikaans (South African version of Dutch) languages in Africa are relics of colonialism, and as such, are residual colonialism. Being residual colonialism, for mutual exclusivists, these languages are part and parcel of the metaphysical empire. Consequently, in the postcolony, to hold on to these White and European languages which were used in the colony and not to return to the African languages of the precolony is to allow oneself to be subjected to the metaphysical empire and consent to be a subject of the metaphysical empire.

On the one hand, the mutual exclusivist-in-chief, Wa Thiong'o (2017), argues that:

> along with the economic and political empires, Europe simultaneously and consciously created empires of the mind through language ideologies and practices, empires in tune with their world view and practical needs. They gave us their accents in exchange for their access to our resources. ... Europe gave Africa the resources of their accent; Africa gave Europe access to the resources of the continent. So when African intellectuals and leaders were busy protecting their borrowed accents, Europe and the West were busy sharpening their instruments for access to the resources of the continent. Accents for Access ... That, unfortunately, is the story of post-colonial Africa.
>
> (s.p.)

On the other hand, the cultural appropriationists-in-chief, Achebe, Soyinka and Adichie, disagree with Wa Thiong'o. For instance, Achebe (1988) argues that there are two positive reasons why Africans use and should use European languages such as the English language (see Ndlovu-Gatsheni, 2018a, p. 112; Omotoso, 1966, p. 145). Firstly, he argues that Africans use and should use the English language for 'political, pragmatic, and convenient' (see Ndlovu-Gatsheni, 2018a, p. 112; see Omotoso, 1966, p. 145) purposes. Secondly, he argues that European languages can serve as successful media of expression of African cultures, thoughts and feelings (see Ndlovu-Gatsheni, 2018a, p. 112; Omotoso, 1966, p. 145).

Achebe's first argument is based on his claim that for complex multi-ethnic and multi-linguistic post-colonial African countries, having a European language such as English, French, Portuguese, Spanish or German as a lingua franca can serve as a source of unity. For instance, for him, for the so-called Anglophone African countries such as Nigeria, the English language is 'a language of national unity' (see Ndlovu-Gatsheni, 2018a, p. 112; Omotoso, 1966, p. 145). Following the same pattern, for the so-called Francophone African countries such as the Democratic Republic of Congo (DRC), the French language is a language of national unity. So too for the so-called Lusophone African countries such as Angola, Mozambique and so on, the Portuguese language is a language of national unity.

If for Achebe the English language is a language of national unity for a country like Nigeria and the French language is a language of national unity for a country like DRC, then one wonders what for him is the language of national unity for North African countries such as Algeria, Libya, Morocco, Tunisia and Egypt, for the Central African country Cameroun and for the Southern African country South Africa.

In North Africa, which language serves as a language of national unity for French- and Arabic-speaking Algeria, Libya, Morocco and Tunisia? Is it the European French, the Middle Eastern Arabic or both the former and the latter? Could it be Arabic because it is the dominant language? Which language serves as a language of national unity for English- and Arabic-speaking Egypt? Is it the European English, the Middle Eastern Arabic or both the former and the latter? Could it be Arabic because it is the dominant language?

In Central Africa, which language serves as a language of national unity for French- and English-speaking Cameroun? Is it French, English or both the former and the latter? Could it be French because it is the dominant language? In Southern Africa, which language serves as a language of national unity for English- and Afrikaans-speaking South Africa? Is it English, Afrikaans or both the former and the latter? Could it be English because it is the dominant language?

The aforementioned questions suggest that Achebe's claim that a European colonial language can serve as a source or medium of national unity for a complex multi-ethnic and multi-linguistic post-colonial African country is not a *fait accompli*. It may seem plausible prima facie, but upon interrogation, it may just be another unconscious acquiescence to the metaphysical empire. What is more plausible is his second argument that European languages such as English and French can 'be successfully used in expressing African culture and African sentiments' (see Ndlovu-Gatsheni, 2018a, p. 112; Omotoso, 1966, p 145).

Achebe is apt to think that

> the use of English enables Africans to be heard at the global level. But I do not think that any African country needs to adopt a European language before it can promote national unity. And we do not have to adopt European languages before we can promote unity

> in Africa. It was this realisation that made Wole Soyinka, after first emphasising 'the importance of choice' in whether to use African languages or European languages, to become 'an advocate for Swahili as a continental language for purposes of enhancement of Pan-African unity.
> (Ndlovu-Gatsheni, 2018a, p. 112, see Omotoso, 1966)

If this realisation made Soyinka, even after first stressing that African writers should have the freedom of choice to use either an African language or a European language as their medium of expression, to 'advocate for Swahili as a continental language for purposes of enhancement of Pan-African unity' (Ndlovu-Gatsheni, 2018a, p. 112; see Omotoso, 1966), then other cultural appropriationists may have to revisit their position.

However, Achebe (1988) even problematises the notion of an African language by questioning what 'exactly' we mean by an African language. He says:

> there has been an impassioned controversy about an African literature in non-African languages. But what is a non-African language? English and French certainly. But what about Arabic? What about Swahili even? Is it then a question of how long the language has been present on African soil? If so, how many years should constitute effective occupation? For me it is again a pragmatic matter. A language spoken by African on African soil, a language in which Africans write, justifies itself.
> (p. 93)

It may not be far-fetched to say that Achebe's position is a negation of conceptual decolonisation. Kwasi Wiredu (1995) posits that decades after flag independence, even when we urgently need decolonisation now more than ever, the post-flag independence period 'does not seem to have brought any indications of a widespread realisation of the need for conceptual decolonisation in African philosophy' (Wiredu, 1995, p. 23). This argument is not limited to the field of philosophy; it is applicable to Achebe's field of literature.

Nevertheless, hypothetically, Achebe can respond that Africans need the adoption of European languages in the same way Africans adopt European technology, medicine and so on. After all, even Wiredu (1980) himself admits that:

> it is as true in Africa as anywhere else that logical, mathematical, analytical, experimental procedures are essential in the quest for the knowledge of, and control over, nature and therefore, in any endeavour to improve the condition of man. Our traditional culture was somewhat wanting in this respect and this is largely responsible for the weaknesses of traditional technology, warfare, architecture, medicine.
> (p. 12)

A plausible counter-argument against the hypothetical Achebe response is that there is a qualitative difference between the adoption of European languages and the adoption of European technology, medicine and so on. While the former is an avenue of imperialism and ultimately ends in social and cultural regression, the latter is an avenue of development and ultimately ends in social and economic progression.

This qualitative difference argument is not far from Frantz Fanon (1963)'s argument that

> when the native is confronted with the colonial order of things, he finds he is in a state of permanent tension. The settler's world is a hostile world, which spurns the native, but at the same time it is a world of which he is envious.
>
> (p. 52)

It is for a reason like this that Jean-Paul Sartre (1963) famously argues that 'the status of "native" is a nervous condition introduced and maintained by the settler among colonised people *with their consent*' (p. 20) (emphasis in original).

Cultural imperialism matters, and it matters a lot because as Fanon (1963) says,

> colonialism is not satisfied merely with holding a people in its grip and emptying the native's brain of all form and content. By a kind of perverted logic, it turns to the past of the oppressed people, and distorts, disfigures and destroys it. This work of devaluing pre-colonial history takes on a dialectical significance today.
>
> (p. 210)

Similar to Fanon's argument, Wa Thiong'o (2009b) argues that European cultural imperialism takes 'a few of the natives, empty their hard disk of previous memory, and download into them a software of European memory' (p. 21). Then these few natives, mimicking Europeans, propagate European cultural imperialism.

Even the term 'native' alone is sufficient grounds for mutual exclusivists to reject the adoption of European languages. According to Mahmood Mamdani (2013), contrary to 'what is commonly thought, native does not designate a condition that is original and authentic' (pp. 2–3). He argues that in contradistinction to the notions of originality and authenticity, 'the native is the creation of the colonial state: colonised, the native is pinned down, localised, thrown out of civilisation as an outcast, confined to custom, and then defined as its product' (Mamdani, 2013).

Like the European usage of the term tribe/tribes rather than ethnicity/ethnicities to describe African societies, the European usage of the term native/natives rather than indigene/indigenes or citizen/citizens to describe Africans and African societies has both negative denotation and connotations. This is part of the reason why an African philosopher like Wiredu calls for conceptual decolonisation and why an African writer like Wa Thiong'o calls for cultural (in general) and linguistic (in particular) decolonisation.

For mutual exclusivists, and it is worth pondering on by cultural appropriationists, the crux of the matter is that, according to Fanon (1963):

> At whatever level we study it … decolonisation is quite simply the replacing of a certain 'species' of men by another 'species' of men. Without any period of transition, there is a total, complete, and absolute substitution. It is true that we could equally well stress the rise of a new nation, the setting up of a new state, its diplomatic relations, and its economic and political trends. But we have precisely chosen to speak of that kind of *tabula rasa* which characterises at the outset all decolonisation. Its unusual importance is that it constitutes, from the very first day, the minimum demands of the colonised. To tell the truth, the proof of success lies in a whole social structure being changed from the bottom up. The extraordinary importance of this change is that it is willed, called for, demanded. The need for this change exists in its crude state, impetuous and compelling, in the consciousness and in the lives of the men and women who are colonised. But the possibility of this change is equally experienced in the form of a terrifying future in the consciousness of another 'species' of men and women: the colonisers.
>
> (pp. 35–36)

A Problem of Worldview?

One may be wondering whether the disagreement between mutual exclusivists and cultural appropriationists is merely a problem of worldview. Prima facie, it is a problem of worldview. But their different worldviews lead them to arrive at different conclusions that fundamentally shape the metaphysical empire debate in opposing ways. Perhaps if both mutual exclusivists and cultural appropriationists have the same consciousness, perception and knowledge of the African experience vis-à-vis European imperialism, their worldviews will not be so fundamentally different.

The Johari Window may be helpful in understanding the differences in the consciousness, perceptions and knowledge of mutual exclusivists and cultural appropriationists vis-à-vis their worldviews. Joseph Luft and Harrington Ingham (1955)'s Johari Window is a psychological analytic device which one can employ to aid her in having a better comprehension or a more comprehensive view of her relationship both with herself and with others. The window has four panes or quadrants, namely Arena, Façade, Blind Spot and Unknown.

The Arena, as the name suggests, is 'open'; it is the 'conscious.' It represents that which both we and others know or perceive about us, that is what we know or perceive about ourselves and which others also know or perceive about us. The Façade, as the name suggests, is 'hidden.' It represents that which we know or perceive about ourselves but others do not know or perceive about us. The Blind Spot, as the name suggests, is also 'hidden.' But there is a qualitative difference between what is hidden in Façade and what is hidden in Blind Spot. While Façade represents what is hidden from others, Blind Spot represents what is hidden from us. Finally, the Unknown is self-explanatory; it represents that which neither we nor others know or perceive about ourselves (see Luft & Ingham, 1955; Luft, 1969; Luft, 1972; Newstrom & Rubenfeld, 1983; Kormanski, 1988; Hase, Davies & Dick, 1999; Emiliano, 2015).

Using the Johari Window, I do not think that it is far-fetched to argue that whether consciously or unconsciously, prima facie, the mutual exclusivism argument is predicated on the belief or fear that appropriating a European colonial language is tantamount to acquiescing to African and Black racial inferiority and European and White racial superiority. For mutual exclusivists, such acquiescence is essentially an acquiescence to the negation of (Black) African identity.

To reiterate, looking at how mutual exclusivists react to the appropriation of European languages and perceive such linguistic appropriation, the importance of perception cannot be overemphasised. Perception matters because, although 'the literature on attitude change … illuminate[s] the ways that discrepant information does in fact alter established views,' consequently, no one should be left with 'the impression that beliefs and images never change'; nevertheless, 'images of others, once established, are hard to dislodge' (Jervis, 2017, p. 10).

The aforementioned perception is even more important in view of, to reiterate, the historical fact that 'the race concept has been used to justify gross forms of injustice: slavery, genocide, colonial subjugation and exploitation, forced segregation and arbitrary civic exclusion, and land and resource expropriation' (Shelby, 2012, p. 337). So, it is safe to say that the mutual exclusivists' belief or fear is not necessarily delusional. Moreover, as Zimitri Erasmus (2017) says:

> All of us live in amongst racialised structures of social meaning. We cannot live outside, above, or beyond the past and the present. Nor can we be outside, above, or beyond the race. Because we are embedded in a racialised world, its ways of seeing and its injustices can be apparent

> to us, and we can be inspired to change it. … In the ongoing process of our liberation we must create openings in the racial house. We must refuse to live by its rules of dominance and its significations.
>
> (p. xxiii)

In the next chapter, we shall see why and how the concepts of race and identity play key roles in the enduring legacies of colonialism which are simultaneously manifested and reflected in ongoing-colonialism, that is, a combination of colonialism, neocolonialism and the metaphysical empire. Since racial identity in particular and identity in general are the principal determinants of where Africans stand on the question of the metaphysical empire and the decolonisation debate, it is important that I explain my conception of both the concept of race and the concept of identity. This explanation is the subject matter of the next chapter.

Essentially, in the next chapter, I shall revisit the conceptual and theoretical framework of the book, the metaphysical empire, which revolves around the phenomenon of identity. I shall introduce and explicate the phenomenon in both its narrow sense (racial identity) and broad sense in order to elucidate the discussion in this chapter and the preceding chapter and to prepare the grounds for the discussion in the remainder of the book. Based on the preliminary discussion of the phenomenon of identity in the next chapter, I shall engage in a detailed analysis of the implications of this phenomenon for the debate on the metaphysical empire in the remainder of this book.

To the above effect, I shall divide the discussion in the next chapter into two parts. In the first part, I shall briefly tease out the concept of race. In the second part, I shall explain the concept of identity, the kind of identity I am concerned about and how this in turn informs the value that mutual exclusivists place on racial identity. Then, I shall explore the preliminary discussion of the chapter in detail in the subsequent chapters.

Bibliography

Abumere, F. A. (2015). *Different Perspectives on Global Justice: A Fusion of Horizons*. Bielefeld, Publication at Bielefeld University (PUB).

Achebe, C. (1988) *Hopes and Impediments: Selected Essays*. New York, Anchor Books.

Ajayi, J. F. A. (1965) *A Thousand Years of West African History: A Handbook for Teachers and Students*, 1st ed. Ibadan, University Press.

Ajayi, J. F. A. (1976) *History of West Africa*. New York, Columbia University Press.

Ekeh, P. P. (1975) Colonialism and the two publics in Africa: A theoretical statement. *Comparative Studies in Society and History* 17 (1), 96–123.

Emiliano, I. (2015) *Heuristic Reasoning: Studies in Applied Philosophy, Epistemology and Rational Ethics*. Cham, Springer.

Erasmus, Z. (2017) *Race Otherwise: Forging New Humanism for South Africa*. Johannesburg, Wits University Press.

Fanon, F. (1963) *The Wretched of the Earth*. New York, Grove Press.

Fanon, F. (1968). *The Wretched of the Earth*. New York, Grove Press.

Hase, S., Davies, A. & Dick, B. (1999) The Johari window and the dark side of organisations. *Ultibase*, 1–5.

Jervis, R. (2017) *Perception and Misperception in International Politics*, rev. ed. Princeton, NJ, Princeton University Press.

Kormanski, L. M. (1988) Using the Johari window to study characterisation. *Journal of Reading* 32 (2), 146–152.

Luft, J. (1969) *Of Human Interaction: The Johari Model*. Palo Alto, CA, National Press.

Luft, J. (1972) *Einfuhrung in die Gruppendynamik*. Stuttgart, Ernst Klett Verlag.

Luft, J. & Ingham, H. (1955) The Johari window, a graphic model of interpersonal awareness. *Proceedings of the Western Training Laboratory in Group Development*, University of California Los Angeles (UCLA), Los Angeles, CA.

Mamdani, M. (2013) *Define and Rule: Native as Political Identity*. Johannesburg, Wits University Press.

Mazrui, A. A. (1978) *Political Values and the Educated Class in Africa*. Berkeley and Los Angeles, CA, University of California Press.

Mazrui, A. A. (1986) *The Africans: A Triple Heritage*. London, BBC Publications.

Ndlovu-Gatsheni, S. J. (2013a) *Coloniality of Power in Postcolonial Africa: Myths of Decolonisation*. Dakar, CODESRIA Books.

Ndlovu-Gatsheni, S. J. (2013b) *Empire, Global Coloniality and African Subjectivity*. New York, Berghahn Books.

Ndlovu-Gatsheni, S. J. (2016) *The Decolonial Mandela: Peace, Justice and the Politics of Life*. New York, Berghahn Books.

Ndlovu-Gatsheni, S. J. (2018a) Metaphysical empire, linguicides and cultural imperialism. *English Academy Review* 35 (2), 96 – 115.

Ndlovu-Gatsheni, S. J. (2018b) *Epistemic Freedom in Africa: Deprovincialisation and Decolonisation*. London, Routledge.

Ndlovu-Gatsheni, S. J. (2019) The struggles for epistemic freedom and the decolonisation of knowledge in Africa. *Webinar Lecture delivered at the Convivial Thinking Collective in collaboration with European Association of Development Research and Training Institutes (EADI), March 12*. https://www.eadi.org/fileadmin/user_upload/EADI/05_Development_Studies/Virtual_Dialogue/EADI_Webinar_12_-_The_Struggles_of_Epistemic_Freedom_and_Decolonization_of_Knowledge_in_Africa__2019-03-12_.pdf

Ndlovu-Gatsheni, S. J. & Zondi, S. (eds) (2016) *Decolonising the University, Knowledge Systems and Disciplines in Africa*. Durham, NC, Carolina Academic Press.

Newstrom, J. W. & Rubenfeld, S. A. (1983) The Johari window: A reconceptualisation. *Developments in Business Simulation and Experiential Learning: Proceedings of the Annual ABSEL Conference*. https://journals.tdl.org/absel/index.php/absel/article/view/2298

Nkrumah, K. (1964) *Consciencism: Philosophy and Ideology for De-Colonisation and Development with Particular Reference to the African Revolution*. New York, Monthly Review Press.

Nkrumah, K. (1965) *Neo-colonialism*. London, Thomas Nelson.

Omotoso, K. (1966) *Achebe or Soyinka: A Study in Contrasts*. Ibadan, Han Zell Publishers.

Quijano, A. (2000). Coloniality of power, Eurocentrism, and Latin America. *Nepantla: Views from the South* 1 (3): 533–579.

Sartre, J-P. (1963) Preface. In: Fanon, F. (ed.) *The Wretched of the Earth*. New York, Grove Press, pp. 7–31.

Shelby, T. (2012) Race. In: Estlund, D. (ed.) *The Oxford Handbook of Political Philosophy*. Oxford, Oxford University Press, pp. 336–353.

Terreblanche, S. (2014). *Western Empires, Christianity and the Inequalities between the West and the Rest 1500–2010*. Johannesburg, Penguin Books.

Wa Ngugi, M. (2018) What decolonising the mind means today. *Literary Hub*, March 23. https://worldpece.org/sites/default/files/artifacts/media/pdf/mukoma_wa_ngugi-_what_decolonizing_the_mind_means_today_literary_hub.pdf

Wa Thiong'o, N. (1986) *Decolonising the Mind: The Politics of Language in African Literature*. Oxford, James Currey.

Wa Thiong'o, N. (1993) *Moving the Centre: The Struggle for Cultural Freedoms*. Oxford, James Currey.

Wa Thiong'o, N. (1997) *Writers in Politics: A Re-Engagement with Issues of Literature and Society*. Oxford, James Currey.

Wa Thiong'o, N. (2009a) *Re-membering Africa*. Nairobi, East African Education Publishers.

Wa Thiong'o, N. (2009b) *Some Thing Torn and New: An African Renaissance*. New York, Basic Civitas Books.

Wa Thiong'o, N. (2012) *Globalectics: Theory and the Politics of Knowing*. New York, Columbia University Press.

Wa Thiong'o, N. (2014) *Resisting Metaphysical Empires: Language as a War Zone*. London, New Beacon Books.

Wa Thiong'o, N. (2016). *Secure the Base: Making Africa Visible in the Globe*. London, Seagull Books.

Wa Thiong'o, N. (2017) African languages – lifting the mask of invisibility. *University World News*. March 10. https://www.universityworldnews.com/post.php?story=20170307102246629

Wiredu, K. (1980) *Philosophy and an African Culture*. Cambridge, Cambridge University Press.

Wiredu, K. (1995) The concept of mind with particular references to the language and thought of the Akan. In: Kwame, S. (ed.) *Readings in African philosophy: An Akan collection*. Lanham, MD, University Press of America, pp. 120–136.

3 Identity, Race and the Metaphysical Empire

On the Concept of Race (A Brief Explanation)

In this chapter, as I mentioned in the preceding chapter, since racial identity in particular and identity in general are the principal determinants of where Africans stand on the question of the metaphysical empire and the decolonization debate, it is important that I explain my conception of both the concept of race and the concept of identity. This explanation is the subject matter of this chapter.

Essentially, in this chapter – again, as I mentioned in the preceding chapter – I shall revisit the conceptual and theoretical framework of the book, the metaphysical empire, which revolves around the phenomenon of identity. I shall introduce and explicate the phenomenon in both its narrow sense (racial identity) and broad sense in order to elucidate the discussion in the previous chapters and to prepare the grounds for the discussion in the remainder of the book. Based on the preliminary discussion of the phenomenon of identity in this chapter, I shall engage in a detailed analysis of the implications of this phenomenon for the debate on the metaphysical empire in the remainder of this book.

To the above effect, I shall divide the discussion in this chapter into two parts. In the first part, I shall briefly tease out the concept of race. In the second part, I shall explain the concept of identity, the kind of identity I am concerned about and how this in turn informs the value that mutual exclusivists place on racial identity. Then, I shall explore the preliminary discussion of this chapter in detail in the subsequent chapters.

Now, shifting focus to discussing race, I shall offer the following brief explanation on the concept of race. I am sanguine about the perspective which holds that race is a social kind and not a natural kind. For this reason, I simultaneously identify with social constructionists who posit that race is a social kind and disagree with naturalists who posit that race is a natural or biological kind.

Furthermore, I disagree with racial sceptics who posit that the concept of race necessarily involves a combination of certain meaningless postulations

DOI: 10.4324/9781003589839-3

and falsehoods. Racial sceptics, in contradistinction to naturalists and social constructionists, disagree that race is a natural kind, biological kind or social kind. They posit that 'the concept of race is intellectually bankrupt, for it necessarily entails several propositions that, given what biologists and anthropologists now know about human variation, are not true' (Shelby, 2012, p. 337; see Appiah, 1996; Blum, 2002; Zack, 2002).

Specifically, racial sceptics posit that if we correctly understand the concept of race, then we will realise that the concept denotes and connotes certain false assumptions. These assumptions, which can be summed up into a four-fold argument, are as follows. The first assumption states that 'there is an underlying essence or cluster of intrinsic properties, inherited through reproduction, that all members of a putative race share and that differentiates a race from all others (racial essentialism)' (Shelby, 2012, p. 337; see Appiah, 1996; Blum, 2002; Zack, 2002).

The second assumption states that 'a person's race determines (to a significant degree) his or her aptitude, culture, or moral character (racial determinism)' (Shelby, 2012, p. 337; see Appiah, 1996; Blum, 2002; Zack, 2002). The third assumption states that 'there is a biological basis for rank ordering racial groupings from superior to inferior (natural racial hierarchy)' (Shelby, 2012, p. 337; see Appiah, 1996; Blum, 2002; Zack, 2002). While the fourth assumption states that 'inter-racial reproduction has deleterious biological consequences (miscegenation as pathological)' (Shelby, 2012, p. 337; see Appiah, 1996; Blum, 2002; Zack, 2002).

Today, there is a consensus, or at least a near consensus, that the aforementioned four-fold claims, otherwise known as classical racialism, are evidently false (Shelby, 2012, p. 337). However, a few decades ago, it was still *normal* for many people to associate with the school of thought that holds that race is a natural kind. Currently, it has become common knowledge that race is a social kind rather than a natural kind or a biological kind. Nevertheless, there are still people who hold on to the false belief that race is a natural kind or a biological kind, which is not surprising because, after all, 'naturalists maintain that racial classification has (at least potentially) taxonomic or explanatory significance in biology' (Shelby, 2012, pp. 337–338; see Andreasen, 1998; Kitcher, 1999; Kitcher, 2007). In spite of their concession that 'there are no racial essences and races are not natural kinds', naturalists are unwavering in their belief that 'races are biological kinds' (Shelby, 2012, pp. 337–338; see Andreasen, 1998; Kitcher, 1999; Kitcher, 2007).

In spite of the fact that 'naturalists do not believe that interracial procreation is harmful,' but because they are convinced that races are biological kinds, they think that some populations, because of geographical barriers, have largely 'been reproductively isolated from other populations for very long periods and that, as a result, some populations manifest certain phenotypic traits at a greater or lesser frequency than other such populations' (Shelby, 2012, pp. 337–338; see Andreasen, 1998; Kitcher, 1999; Kitcher, 2007). Consequently, naturalists think that a race is 'a relatively inbred lineage of common geographical origin whose members are identifiable by their visible inherited physical traits' (Shelby, 2012, pp. 337–338). If the naturalists are right, then '"real races" do not correspond to, and in fact may undermine, our commonsense folk categories of racial classification (e.g., "black" and "white")' (Shelby, 2012, pp. 337–338; see Andreasen, 1998; Kitcher, 1999; Kitcher, 2007). (emphasis in original).

In contradistinction to naturalists, social constructionists posit that race is socially constructed. As far as social constructionists are concerned, in spite of the fact that race is not biologically important, it 'is a meaningful social category that divides humans into subgroups for both illegitimate and legitimate social purposes' (Shelby, 2012, p. 338; see Goldberg, 1993; Haslanger, 2000; Mills, 1998; Sundstrom, 2002; Taylor, 2004). For this reason, social constructionists pivot from the theorisation on, and conceptualisation of, race as a biological kind to the theorisation on, and conceptualisation of, race as a social kind. Put differently, for social constructionists, race is a social kind rather than a biological kind, and race has to do with social relations rather than biology (Shelby, 2012, p. 338; see Goldberg, 1993; Haslanger, 2000; Mills, 1998; Sundstrom, 2002; Taylor, 2004).

If this assertion by social constructionists is correct, then 'the groups that we now call "races" were created by a set of historically specific and ever-changing social practices' (Shelby, 2012, p. 338) (emphasis in original). From a social constructionist perspective, Ronald Chisom and Michael Washington (1997) define race as 'a specious classification of human beings created by Europeans (whites) which assigns human worth and social status using "white" as the model of humanity and the height of human achievement for the purpose of establishing and maintaining privilege and power' (pp. 30–31) (emphasis in original). Chisom and Washington's definition and assertion alert us to the danger of White supremacy. White supremacy is dangerous because it

> is an historically based, institutionally perpetuated system of exploitation and oppression of continents, nations and peoples of colour by white peoples and nations of the European continent, for the purpose of maintaining and defending a system of wealth, power and privilege.
>
> (Chisom & Washington, 1997, pp. 30–31)

The aforementioned description of White supremacy and its characteristics can only be strange to us or surprise us when we forget the historical invention of the notion of 'White' itself as a racial category. The notion of 'White' as a racial category which refers to White people was invented in the seventeenth century by chattel slave owners and colonialists in Virginia (United States of America) (Chisom & Washington, 1997, pp. 30–31; see Adair & Powell, 1988, p. 17.). When the notion of 'White' was first used, it was used such as Christian, Englishman and so on, and:

> to distinguish European colonists from Africans and indigenous peoples. European colonial powers established white as a legal concept after Bacon's Rebellion in 1676 during which indentured servants of European and African descent had united against the colonial elite. The legal distinction of white separated the servant class on the basis of skin colour and continental origin.
>
> (Chisom & Washington, 1997, pp. 30–31; see Adair & Powell, 1988, p. 17)

Essentially, the invention of '"white" meant giving privileges to some, while denying them to others with the justification of biological and social inferiority' (Chisom & Washington, 1997, pp. 30–31) (emphasis in original). Deeming some to be worthy of certain privileges and deeming others to be unworthy of those privileges, and giving those privileges to the former and denying the latter those privileges based on biological and social superiority and inferiority categorisation, is exactly what White supremacy is about. By treating White people as a superior and privileged people and treating non-White people as an inferior and non-privileged people, White supremacy benefits the former at the expense of the latter.

Narrating her personal experience as a White person, Peggy Macintosh (1989) says, 'I had been taught about racism that puts others at a disadvantage, but had been taught not to see one of its corollary aspects, white privilege, which puts me at an advantage' (s.p.). Consequently, Macintosh categorically states that, 'White privilege is an invisible package of unearned assets which I can count on cashing in every day, but about which I was meant to remain oblivious' (Macintosh, 1989, s.p.). Macintosh's statement points us to the fact that White privilege is at once a historical and current phenomenon. As a historical and current phenomenon, White privilege 'refers to whites' historical and contemporary advantages in access to quality education, decent jobs and livable wages, homeownership, retirement benefits, wealth and so on' (Macintosh, 1989, s.p.).

Specifically, as a historical phenomenon, White privilege has to do with the privileges that have accrued to White people by virtue of being White and to the detriment of non-White people by virtue of them being non-White. In other words, as a historical phenomenon,

> White privilege is an historically based, institutionally perpetuated system of: (1) Preferential prejudice for and treatment of white people based solely on their skin colour and/or ancestral origin from Europe;

> and (2) Exemption from racial and/or national oppression based on skin colour and/or ancestral origin from Africa, Asia, the Americas and the Arab world.
>
> (Macintosh, 1989, s.p.)

Virginia Harris and Trinity Ordoña (1990) use the case of the USA to exemplify the aforementioned description of White privilege as a historical phenomenon. In the USA, according to Harris and Ordoña (1990), 'White peoples were exempt from slavery, land grab and genocide, the first forms of white privilege' (p. 310). After all, American

> institutions and culture (economic, legal, military, political, educational, entertainment, familial and religious) privilege peoples from Europe over peoples from the Americas, Africa, Asia and the Arab world. In a white supremacy system, white privilege and racial oppression are two sides of the same coin.
>
> (Chisom & Washington, 1997, pp. 30–31; see Adair & Powell, 1988, p. 17)

Despite the fact that White privilege benefits White people at the expense of non-White people, and for the purpose of disguising White privilege and securing and perpetuating its benefits, some White people argue that there is no such thing as White privilege. They did not stop there. They go on to argue that instead of White privilege, what actually exists is non-White privilege. In short, they argue that rather than White racism, what we actually have is anti-White racism. In other words, they think or argue that rather than the usual racism, what we have is reverse racism.

Essentially, reverse racism is a mechanism through which the beneficiaries of White privilege (namely White people) accuse those who are disadvantaged by White privilege (namely non- White people) of benefiting from non-White privilege at the expense of White people. In other words, White people invented and deployed the notion of reverse racism in order 'to deny their white privilege. Those in denial use the term reverse racism to refer to hostile behaviour by people of colour toward whites, and to affirmative action policies, which allegedly give "preferential treatment" to people of colour over whites' (Lawrence & Keleher, 2004, s.p.) (emphasis in original).

The postulations of reverse racism are evidently false. Both historically and currently, there is no piece of evidence to back up the claims of reverse racism. Given the trajectory of world history and world politics, and the nature of domestic politics in our world both in the past and in the present, reverse racism is simultaneously practicably impossible and theoretically implausible. My counter-claim about the invalidity and falsity of the claims of reverse racism is not a mere academic exercise. The validity and truth value of my counter-claim can be seen in Africa (looking at South Africa, Zimbabwe and so on), in North America (looking at the USA and Canada), in Europe (looking at the United Kingdom, France and so on), in Australasia (looking at Australia and New Zealand), in South America (looking at Argentina, Brazil and so on) or anywhere for that matter.

This brief explanation of the concept of race is vital to comprehending the metaphysical empire and appreciating the contrasting positions on the metaphysical empire because in the context of the metaphysical empire, even linguistic identity itself and cultural identity do not stand *sui generis*, they stand in relation to racial identity and as subsets of identity in general. It is for this reason that all the analyses and narratives in the book are woven together through the concept of identity in general and racial identity in particular. So, having briefly introduced the phenomenon of racial identity (identity narrowly construed as race) in this sub-chapter, in the next sub-chapter I shall introduce the phenomenon of identity (identity broadly construed). To do this, I shall conduct my narrative by reviewing the state of the art of the concept of identity in Africa (Abumere, 2022), which was the *locus* of empire and is the subject of the metaphysical empire in question.

The Problem of Identity

Cressida Heyes (2020) succinctly and rightly notes that 'identity has become indispensable to contemporary political discourse' (sec. 1). Apart from being indispensable, identity, Heyes (2020) notes, also 'has troubling implications for models of the self, political inclusiveness, and our possibilities for solidarity and resistance' (sec. 1). On his part, Ted Hopf (1998) argues that, without identity, we will be living in a world that lacks order, stability and peace. In Hopf (1998)'s words, our world will be a 'world of chaos, a world of pervasive and irremediable uncertainty, a world much more dangerous than anarchy' (p. 175). While Hopf is certainly right that identity is helpful in bringing about some certainty in our world, his statement is not the whole truth. Identity is a double-edged sword; it also leads to chaos and conflicts.

According to David Campbell (1992), 'identity is an inescapable dimension of being. Nobody could be without it' (p. 9). While according to Felix Berenskoetter (2017), 'identities manifest our ontology of the international and play a central role in politics' (p. 1). Identity does not only manifest our ontology of the international, it also manifests our ontology of the local or domestic. So, even though Anthony Burke (2006) is correct to say that 'there is … no world politics without identity, no people, no states, no international system' (p. 394), I must add that there is no domestic politics without identity. So too although Bruce Cronin (1999) says that 'identities provide a frame of reference from which political leaders can initiate, maintain, and structure their relationships with other states' (p. 18), one can add that identities provide a frame of reference from which individuals and groups can initiate, maintain and structure their relationships with other individuals, groups, the government and even the state itself.

Since my focus is on a particular identity, my discussion on identity shall revolve around that particular identity. Consequently, I shall not delve into the general discourse on identity even though I shall draw insights from such discourse. My focus is on African identity, and the discussion that follows should be seen purely within the context of African philosophical conceptions of identity in contradistinction to non-African philosophical conceptions of identities such as Western philosophical conception of identity, Chinese philosophical conception of identity, the broader Asian philosophical conception of identity and so on.

In my reliance on African philosophical conceptions of identity, I will draw insight from both African philosophers and non-philosophers. It is obvious why I will draw insights from the former – they are African philosophers who have thought, or who are thinking, about African identities. In the case of the latter, although they are not philosophers, their socio-cultural ideas about African identities which they expressed in different forms, both fiction and non-fiction – for instance, *fictional* literature and *non-fictional* writings, commentaries and interviews in the case of Chinua Achebe, Wole Soyinka, Ngugi Wa Thiong'o and so on – are no less philosophical than the ideas of African philosophers which were or are expressed in philosophical forms.

Given this two-fold statement that (i) I will draw insights from both African philosophers and non-philosophers and (ii) the ideas of the latter are no less philosophical than the ideas of the former, in my discussion on identity, my reliance on African conceptions of identity or identities is essentially or remains a reliance on African philosophical conceptions of identities – here, 'philosophical' is construed broadly to include both former or professional philosophy and non-former or non-professional philosophy.

In my discussion on African identities, my decision to rely on African *philosophical* conceptions of identity (note that the emphasis is on *philosophical*) rather than, say, African anthropological conceptions of identity, African sociological conceptions of identity, African political conceptions of identity and so on is not only based on the fact that this is a philosophical book, specifically an African philosophy book. It is also based on the fact that 'African conceptions of identity are particularly espoused by African thinkers' (Abumere, 2023, p. 8; see Abumere, 2022). For this reason, I will especially

> rely on postcolonial African thinkers to tease out the concept of identity. So, the thoughts of thinkers such as Frantz Fanon (although he is

> not continental African, as a diasporic African he is an African in a Pan-Africanist sense), Chinua Achebe, Kwame Gyekye, Kwasi Wiredu, Achille Mbembe, Kwame Anthony Appiah and Achie Mafeje pervade my narrative on the concept of identity.
>
> (Abumere, 2023, p. 8)

To understand African philosophical conceptions of identity or identities, we need to know what African philosophers take the fundamental objective of philosophy – whether African philosophy, non-African philosopher or philosophy in general – to be. Kwame Gyekye (1995) notably asserts that philosophy has a four-fold fundamental objective. Outlining the fundamental objectives in no particular order of hierarchy or lexicon, the fundamental objectives are as follows.

In the first fundamental objective, he postulates that a fundamental objective of philosophy is the provision of 'a basic system of beliefs that will guide peoples' lives' (Abumere, 2023, p. 8; see Gyekye, 1995, p. 23). In the second fundamental objective, he postulates that a fundamental objective of philosophy is the determination of 'the nature of human values and how these values can be realised concretely in human societies' (Gyekye, 1995, p. 23).

In the third fundamental objective, he postulates that a fundamental objective of philosophy is the provision of 'conceptual interpretations and analysis of [human] experience, necessarily doing so not only by responding to the basic issues and problems generated by that experience but also by suggesting new or alternative ways of thought and action' (p. 24). Note that, for Gyekye, this third fundamental objective of philosophy becomes possible through speculation about 'the whole range of human experience' (p. 23).

Following from the first, second and third fundamental objectives, in the fourth fundamental objective, he postulates that a fundamental objective of philosophy is the provision of 'conceptual responses to the problems posed in any given epoch for a given society or culture' (p. 27). Gyekye's fundamental objectives of philosophy are a broad conception of the fundamental objective(s) of philosophy. While philosophy in general and all philosophies share those fundamental objectives, in addition, every group of people has its own specific or special philosophical objectives. This is because

> spatio-temporal circumstances make the specific aim(s) of philosophy for one group of people different from the specific aim(s) of philosophy for another group of people. For example, one would expect the specific aim(s) of philosophy for Africans, given their spatio-temporal circumstances to be substantially different from the aim(s) of philosophy for White people.
>
> (Abumere, 2023, p. 8)

Within the aforementioned context, for instance, Frantz Fanon (1967)'s famous analysis of the predicament of the African and Black person points us to a reason why the fundamental objectives of African philosophy are, can or should be unique. Just as the predicament is unique to the African and Black person, and just as the experience and life-world of the African and Black person is unique, so too the fundamental objectives of the philosophy that reflects on such predicament, experience and life-world are unique.

Fanon (1967) notes that the African and Black person has one dimension in her relationship with her fellow African and Black person while at the same time having a different dimension in her relationship with the White person. He observes that the African and Black person perceives herself to be inferior to the White person. 'But since such inferiority/superiority complex is absent in Black people's perception of themselves in relation to other Black people, their behaviour in their relationship and interaction with one another is different from their behaviour when they interact with White people' (Abumere, 2023, p. 8).

In extreme cases, the African and Black person perceives herself to be inferior to the White person while at the same time perceiving her fellow African and Black person to be inferior to her. Consequently, her worldview is characterised by a dualistic inferiority/superiority complex, and this inferiority/superiority complex determines what she thinks about Africans or Black people and White people, and how she relates and interacts with them.

In the aforementioned inferiority/superiority complex, on the one hand, the African and Black person thinks that she is inferior to the White person because she has internalised the White person's projection of the African or Black person as a non-human or lesser human and the White person as a human or full human. On the other hand, the African or Black person thinks that she is superior to her fellow African or Black person because she imitates and aspires to be like the White person.

According to Fanon (1967), it is indisputable that the aforementioned self-division is directly caused by the colonial conquest and oppression of the African and Black person by the White person (p. 8). Consequently,

> on the one hand, while emancipation from colonialist subjugation is a specific aim of philosophy for Black people, it is not a specific aim of philosophy for White people. On the other hand, while the Fanonian self-division (assuming Fanon is right) is part of the identity of Black people, it is not part of the identity of White people.
>
> (Abumere, 2023, p. 8)

The Fanonian self-division reflects 'the spatio-temporal circumstances of the African people both in terms of internal dynamics (internal interactions and relations in Africa) and external dynamics (external interactions and relations between Africa and the rest of the world) both historically and presently' (Abumere, 2023, p. 8; see Abumere 2022). Given such spatio-temporal circumstances, Achie Mafeje (2008 [2000]) calls on Africans to cultivate an African identity that embodies the values of what he refers to as new Pan-Africanism. In his words, we need 'a new Pan-Africanism that brooks neither external dependence nor internal authoritarianism and social deprivation' (p. 113).

Similarly, that is given the aforementioned spatio-temporal circumstances and along the line of Mafeje's call, Kwasi Wiredu and Kwame Gyekye (1992), even more than one and half decades before Mafeje, advise African philosophers to focus on the things that matter to the continent and its people. Wiredu and Gyekye (1992) say that 'philosophers belonging to a given culture or era or tradition select those concepts or clusters of concepts that, for one reason or another, matter most and that therefore are brought to the fore in their analysis' (p. 7). Given this tradition in philosophy of philosophers focusing on things that matter to their people and places, and in view of the aforementioned spatio-temporal circumstances, Wiredu and Gyekye (1992) notify African philosophers that 'this is the time when there is the maximum need to study African traditional philosophy' (p. 98).

I would even go beyond Wiredu and Gyekye's assertion that this is the time to study African philosophy to say that this is the time to focus specifically on African political philosophy (Abumere, 2022). In their study of African political philosophy, African political philosophers should be conscious that 'the starting points, the organising concepts and categories' of current African political philosophy must 'be extracted from the cultural, linguistic, and historical background of African peoples if that philosophy is to have relevance and meaning for the people, if it is to enrich their lives' (Gyekye, 1995, pp. 33, 42).

I think that if any theorisation about the metaphysical empire is to be relevant to Africans, then such theorisation must be concerned with an African *Zeitgeist* which I think identity is. When discussing *Zeitgeist*, it is common for people to refer to *the Zeitgeist* rather than *a Zeitgeist*. Put differently, when discussing *Zeitgeist*, people commonly deploy the definite article 'the' instead of the indefinite article 'a' or 'an' to prefix *Zeitgeist* (Abumere, 2023, p. 9). Given the tight relationship that exists between subjectivity and temporality in current Africa, it is plausible to argue that 'identity is a *Zeitgeist* on the African continent because complex historical and current experiences indicate that the identity puzzle is one of the fundamental puzzles African philosophers are determined to solve' (p. 10).

In order to resolve the identity puzzle, or at least in order to attempt to resolve the puzzle, it is vital to understand that identity is a *Zeitgeist* on the African continent. Then, resolving the puzzle itself is necessary for different reasons chief among which is that identity has been weaponised both by oppressors to oppress others and by the oppressed to contextualise the oppression they suffer in the hands of the oppressors (Mbembe, 2019, s.p.; Abumere 2022). As Mbembe (2019) says,

> identity is increasingly used both as a weapon to further brutalise the weakest in our midst and as a leverage to claim a status of pure or authentic victim. To have been brutalised or to have been victimised, in turn, is increasingly seen as the most potent way to claim one's rights or one's access to care, justice, redress or reparation.
>
> (s.p.)

Ordinarily, in order to resolve the identity puzzle, there are two ways to approach it. The first way is to approach it as a category of practice, while the second way is to approach it as a category of analysis (Brubaker & Cooper, 2000). Ordinarily, people opt either for the former or for the latter. Generally, neither the former nor the latter is superior or inferior as such in comparative terms. While the former is more suitable for practical purposes, the latter is more suitable for theoretical purposes.

Since I am more concerned about theoretical analysis than practicable policies, one would expect that I would opt for the category of analysis rather than the category of practice. However, the category of practice, rather than the category of analysis, is more suitable for my purpose because even though this is not a policy book with policy prescriptions, I am concerned about the practice of identity in the everyday life of the African person. Nevertheless, opting for the category of practice approach does not necessarily mean that I am at the same discounting the category of analysis approach. What it means is that my emphasis is on the category of practice approach rather than the category of analysis approach. So, while deploying the category of practice approach to resolve the identity puzzle, I will deploy 'the category of analysis approach to complement the category of practice approach (what I can lightly refer to as a supplementary approach)' (Abumere, 2023, p. 10).

In my supplementary approach, I will heed Rogers Brubaker and Frederick Cooper (2000)'s advice that in the attempt to resolve the identity puzzle, when using either the category of practice approach or the category of analysis approach, we should not misconstrue the former for the latter and vice versa (p. 5). Furthermore, in my supplementary approach, I will heed Zoe Bray (2008)'s advice not to treat identity in a preconceived manner since both the preconception of identity and the treatment of identity in a preconceived manner blind us from seeing the true picture of identity. According to Bray (2008), 'preconceived treatment of identity is very common amongst researchers who continue to take it for granted as comprising a specific array of characteristics, rather than considering the mechanisms by which the concept is crystallised as reality' (p. 303).

By using a supplementary approach in the resolution of the identity puzzle, I guard against a reductionist approach to identity. According to Amartya Sen (2007), a reductionist approach to identity can be either identity disregard or singular affiliation (p. 20). In his words:

> two different types of reductionism seem to abound in the formal literature of social and economic analysis. One may be called 'identity disregard,' and it takes the form of ignoring, or neglecting altogether, the influence of any sense of identity with others, on what we value and how we behave .... In contrast with 'identity disregard,' there is a different kind of reductionism, which we may call 'singular affiliation,' which takes the form of assuming that any person preeminently belongs, for all practical purposes, to one collectivity only.
>
> (p. 20) (emphasis in original)

One thing, among many, which identity disregard and singular affiliation point out to us is that the concept of identity fits what W.B. Gallie (1956) refers to as essentially contested concept. Essentially contested concepts denote different things to different people; therefore, people are usually disagreed on what exactly such concepts mean (p. 169). In other words, concepts are said to be essentially contested when they do not have a canonical meaning. Like every other concept, essentially contested concepts have their etymological meanings. However, along the line, that is, in the course of usage over time or as time passes by, users discard the etymological meanings of essentially contested concepts or only some users maintain the etymological meanings while others formulate new meanings for the concepts. Simply put, essentially contested concepts represent one thing to user A, another thing to user B, may represent yet another thing to user C and so on, and none of these representations is deemed to be the acceptable meaning of such concepts (Abumere, 2019, p. 1).

In view of the aforementioned definition of essentially contested concept, it is very easy to understand why identity is an essentially contested concept. This is because

> as an essentially contested concept, or at least as a seemingly essentially contested concept, identity can be understood in positive or moral sense, negative or immoral sense, or neutral or amoral sense. No matter in which of these senses one understands identity, identity can be employed either for reactionary purposes or for progressive purposes or for both purposes.
>
> (Abumere, 2023, p. 11)

Being one of the foremost theorists of identity, both identity in general and African identity in particular, Kwame Anthony Appiah's understanding of identity in general and African identity in particular sheds light on why identity is an essentially contested concept. More importantly, Appiah's understanding of identity gives us helpful insights into how to resolve the identity puzzle. Appiah (1992) notably understands identity to be 'a coalescence of mutually responsive (if sometimes conflicting) modes of conduct, habits of thought, and patterns of evaluation; in short, a coherent kind of human social psychology' (p. 174).

Furthermore, Appiah (1992) notes that 'the African identity is, for its bearers, only one among many. Like all identities, institutionalised before anyone has permanently fixed a single meaning for them' (p. 177). What Appiah (1992) simply means is that anyone who identifies as an African knows, and is conscious of, the fact that 'being African is … one among other salient modes of being, all of which have to be constantly fought for and rethought' (p. 177).

Like Appiah, and exactly a decade after Appiah expressed the aforementioned view on African identity, Achille Mbembe (2002) posited that every African 'can imagine and choose what makes him or her an African' (p. 258). However, there is a difference between Appiah and Mbembe or between Appiah's thought and Mbembe's thought. For Appiah (1992), tribal identity (put differently, ethnic identity) is one of the most important identities, if not the most important identity, on the African continent. This is because, in Appiah (1992)'s opinion, tribal identity (or ethnic identity) 'provides one of the most useful models for … rethinking' African identity as 'one among other salient modes of being, all of which have to be constantly fought for and rethought' (p. 177). In other words, in Appiah (1992)'s opinion, tribal identity (or ethnic identity) 'is a model that draws on other identities central to contemporary life in the subcontinent, namely, the constantly shifting redefinition of 'tribal' identities to meet the economic and political exigencies of the modern world' (p. 177). But for Mbembe (2002), rather than tribes or ethnicities, 'the state of war in contemporary Africa should, in fact, be conceived of as a general cultural experience that shapes identities, just as the family, the school, and other social institutions do' (p. 267).

Between Mbembe's state of war postulation and Appiah's tribal identity postulation, the latter seems to be more popular. For instance, even a decade before Appiah's postulation, one of the finest thinkers of identity on the African continent, Chinua Achebe (1982), made a similar postulation that is based on tribe or ethnicity. Since 'the tribal identity model claim was made ten years earlier by Chinua Achebe before Appiah reiterated it ten years later' (Abumere, 2023, p. 11), it is plausible to argue that 'Appiah's claim seems to be a corroboration of Achebe's claim' (p. 11). Put differently, 'Appiah's claim that tribal identity provides one of the most useful models for rethinking identity in Africa … seems to corroborate

Achebe's' (p. 11) in which he describes himself by emphasising his Ibo ethnicity.

In Achebe (1982)'s self-description, he makes the following categorical statement: 'I'm an Ibo writer, because this is my *basic* culture' (s.p.) (emphasis mine). His emphasis on his Ibo identity is clear and distinct even though he later broadened his self-description to include other identities. In other words, he sees himself, first and foremost, as an Ibo even though he 'does not restrict his self-description to the Ibo/Igbo culture, that is, he does not limit his identity to the Ibo/Igbo culture' (Abumere, 2023, p. 11). In his self-description, after 'describing himself as an Ibo writer and describing his Ibo identity as his basic culture [... Achebe] also describes himself as a Nigerian, African and Black' (p. 11). In his words, he is not only an Ibo, but he is also a 'Nigerian, African and a writer ... no, black first, then a writer' (Achebe, 1982, s.p.).

Looking as his multiple identities – Ibo, Nigerian, African, Black and writer – Achebe (1982) says that:

> Each of these identities does call for a certain kind of commitment on my part. I must see what it is to be black – and this means being sufficiently intelligent to know how the world is moving and how the black people fare in the world. This is what it means to be black. Or an African – the same: what does Africa mean to the world? When you see an African what does it mean to a white man?
>
> (s.p.)

Ostensibly, Achebe's multiple identities include the Ibo ethnic and cultural identity, the Nigerian national identity, the African regional or continental identity, the Black racial identity and the writer professional identity. Put differently, Achebe subjectively conceives of himself as someone who possesses a five-fold identity and wants to be objectively seen as someone who possesses such a five-fold identity (Abumere, 2022). But note that in terms of the arrangement of the identities in order of hierarchy or lexicon:

> Ibo comes first, Nigerian comes second, African comes third, Black comes fourth and writer comes fifth. His identity as an African only comes before his identities as Black and writer but comes after his identities as Ibo and Nigerian. That Achebe gives precedence to his identities as Ibo and Nigerian over his identity as an African (this does not in any way suggest that he thinks the various identities are mutually exclusive) may be a function of the trajectory of the formation of the African identity understood in its singularity, that is as a singular identity, as opposed to African identities understood in their plurality, that is as plural identities.
>
> (Abumere, 2023, p. 12)

The distinction between African identity understood in its singularity and African identities understood in their pluralities is at the heart of the evolution of African identity itself, the conception of such identity in theory and the everyday experience of such identity in practice. Appiah (1992), once again, notes that

> to speak of an African identity in the nineteenth century … would have been 'to give to aery nothing a local habitation and a name.' Yet there is no doubt that now, a century later, an African identity is coming into being … this identity is a new thing; … it is the product of a history.
>
> (p. 174) (emphasis in original)

In view of the aforementioned claim by Appiah, there are likely two different lived experiences of the African identity and we will likely have two different perceptions of the state of African identity: On the one hand, there are likely a nineteenth-century lived experience of the African identity and a late twentieth-century lived experience of the African identity; on the other hand, we will likely have one perception of the state of African identity in the nineteenth century and another perception of the state of African identity in the late twentieth century. We will probably suppose that 'the nineteenth century African identity was in a liquid form, but by late twentieth century the African identity was evolving from its liquid form to a solid form' (Abumere, 2023, p. 12).

What is evident, or at least what we can deduce, from the distinction between nineteenth-century African identity and late twentieth-century African identity is that:

> On the one hand, the African identity in the twenty-first century (specifically this early twenty-first century) is apparently, and I dare say evidently, stronger than the African identity in the nineteenth century. On the other hand, it is difficult to say whether the identity is still in a liquid state, or has transformed into a solid state or it is still transforming from a liquid state to a solid state. Appiah's argument does not tell us when the solidification of the African identity will happen; however it suggests that in its liquid state there are only pluralities of African identities and in its solid state there will be a singularity of African identity.
>
> (Abumere, 2023, p. 12)

In this early twenty-first century and in the near future, given the trajectory of African identity, I do not see any solid African identity replacing liquid African identities; that is, I do not see any singular African identity replacing plural African identities. Since history is retrospective rather than prospective, the past might diverge from the future. But what the present – standing between the past and the future – tells us is that the transformation of African identity from a liquid state to a solid state and from plurality to singularity is probably unlikely in the near future. In the distant future, such transformation may be possible both in theory and in practice, but for now, it may be possible in theory but not in practice.

I think that it does not matter whether there is a solid African identity or liquid African identity or whether there is a singular African identity or there are plural African identities. What matters is whether a solid African identity can co-exist with a liquid African identity or whether a singular African identity can co-exist with plural African identities. I think that a singular African identity does not need to displace or replace plural African identities. It is simultaneously theoretically plausible and practicably possible for us to have a situation whereby rather than displacing or replacing plural African identities, a singular African identity is either superimposed on plural African identities or both the former and the latter are co-existing. In other words:

> the existing plurality of identities will not evolve into a singular identity; that is, it will not necessarily be replaced by a singular identity. Rather, both will coexist in a condition whereby in a metaphysical sense the singular identity is the universal while the plural identities are the particulars, or in a taxonomic ranking, the singular identity is the genus while the plural identities are the species, or in an ordinary language sense, the singular identity represents the general identity while the plural identity represents specific identities.
>
> (Abumere, 2022, s.p.)

Appiah (1992) captures the essence of the co-existence of a singular African identity with plural African identities when, translating and interpreting an Akan proverb, he says that although we are all Africans, 'each of us…belongs to a group with its own customs' (p. 180). So, for Appiah (1992), the consequence of accepting that we can still retain our pluralistic African identities even when we are all gathered under the umbrella of a singular African identity is that

> to accept that Africa can be in these ways a usable identity is not to forget that all of us belong to multifarious communities with their local customs; it is not to dream of a single African state and to forget the complexly different trajectories of the continent's so many languages and cultures.
>
> (p. 180)

Appiah and Achebe agree on this point that a singular African identity can co-exist with plural African identities. Given that Achebe's discussion on the matter came exactly ten years before Appiah's, we might be right to say that the latter took a cue from the former. Whether Appiah took his cue from Achebe or not, and whether Appiah arrived at his conclusion independently of Achebe's view on the matter, what matters is that two of the most prominent African thinkers of identity are agreed that a singular African identity can co-exist with plural African identities. According to Achebe (1982):

> It is, of course, true that the African identity is still in the making. There isn't a final identity that is African. But, at the same time, there is an identity coming into existence. And it has a certain context and a certain meaning. Because if somebody meets me, say, in a shop in Cambridge [England], he says 'Are you from Africa?' Which means that Africa means something to some people. Each of these tags has a meaning, and a penalty and a responsibility. All these tags, unfortunately for the black man, are tags of disability.
>
> (s.p.) (emphasis in original)

Like every human identity, the singular African identity and plural African identities are social kinds rather than natural kinds. In other words, they are socially constructed. The fact that African identities are socially constructed means that, like every human identity, they contain histories, prejudices, conjectures and so on. Where and when human identities contain histories, they are closer to reality than they are to myth. But where and when they contain prejudices, conjectures and other presuppositions, they are closer to myth than they are to reality. Such presuppositions play different roles and have different meanings and names in different contexts: In the context of history, such presuppositions are considered to be myths; in the context of religion, they are considered to be heresies; and in the context of science, they are considered to be magic (Appiah 1992, p. 174).

Once we understand that African identities, like every other human identity, are socially constructed, and if we understand that socially constructed identities can be re-constructed to exclude old aspects, to include new aspects or to do both, then we will understand that in view of the metaphysical empire contention between mutual exclusivists and cultural appropriationists, accommodative decolonisation is possible. While the sixth and final chapter of this book is dedicated to discussing the possibility and plausibility of accommodative decolonisation, I want to quickly mention here that the aforementioned accommodative decolonisation is possible and plausible as long as we are agreed that 'invented histories, invented biologies, invented cultural affinities come with every identity; each is a kind of role that has to be scripted, structured by conventions of narrative to which the world never quite manages to conform' (p. 174).

Whether an identity is deep or shallow depends on whether it is socially constructed and historical or not, and if socially constructed and historical, how and why it is socially constructed and to what extent it is historical.

> The kind of histories invented and the way they are invented, the kind of biologies invented and the ways they are invented and the kind of cultural affinities invented and the way they are invented determine whether a human identity is deep, shallow or middle-of-the-road between the former and the latter.
>
> (Abumere, 2023, pp. 13–14)

It is common to assume that identities that have existed for a long period of time are deep while identities that have existed for a short period of time are shallow. In other words, it is common to assume that, comparatively, identities that have existed for a longer period of time are deeper than identities that have existed for a shorter period of time, and conversely identities that have existed for a shorter period of time are shallower than identities that have existed for a longer period of time. For this reason, people usually think that

> in terms of time period, the longer one is aware or conscious of his or her identity, the deeper such identity is. Conversely, the shorter one is aware or conscious of his or her identity, the shallower his or her identity is.
>
> (p. 14)

However, Achebe (1982) tells us that 'the duration of awareness, of consciousness of an identity, has really very little to do with how deep it is. You can suddenly become aware of an identity which you have been suffering from for a long time without knowing' (s.p.).

Using his Ibo ethnic identity, Achebe attempts to prove his point that the length of time one has been aware or conscious of her socially constructed identity does not determine how deep or shallow her socially constructed identity is. He says that in the course of their long history, the Ibo people only began to see themselves and refer to themselves as Ibo recently. Before then, they saw themselves not as the larger ethnic group called Ibo, but as small ethnic and sub-ethnic groups and clans from different clans, villages, towns and cities with different identities and different names. He goes on to say that:

> In fact, in some place 'Igbo' was a word of abuse; they were the 'other' people, down in the bush. And yet, after the experience of the Biafran War, during a period of two years, it became a very powerful consciousness. But it was real all the time. They all spoke the same language, called 'Igbo,' even though they were not using that identity in

> any way. But the moment came when this identity became very very powerful ... and over a very short period.
>
> (s.p.) (emphasis in original)

There is a three-fold lesson that we can learn from what Achebe said about the Ibo. These lessons are not only vital to our comprehension of African identities; they are also vital to the comprehension of human identities in general or any socially constructed identity for that matter (Abumere, 2023). The first lesson is a lesson of indication in which his analysis of Ibo ethnic identity serves as the indicator. The second lesson is a lesson of demonstration in which his analysis serves as the demonstrator, while the third lesson is a lesson of guidance in which his analysis serves as the guide.

In the first lesson, his analysis indicates, and we learn, that socially constructed identities 'are complex and multiple and grow out of a history of changing responses to economic, political, and cultural forces, almost always in opposition to other identities' (Appiah, 1992, p. 178). In the second lesson, his analysis demonstrates, and we see, that socially constructed identities can blossom regardless of our failure to recognise where they originated from, how they originated and why they originated. In other words, socially constructed identities blossom even though we fail, or even when we fail, to recognise that they are rooted in myths and falsehoods (p. 178).

In the third lesson, his analysis guides us to internalising the consequences of the first and second lessons. In view of the first and second lessons, we become aware that while there may be ample room for reason in the study of identities and even in the management of identities, such ample room does not exist for reason in the construction of identities (p. 178). Consequently, according to Appiah (1992),

> one temptation, then, for those who see the centrality of these fictions in our lives, is to leave reason behind: to celebrate and endorse those identities that seem at the moment to offer the best hope of advancing our other goals, and to keep silent about the lies and the myths.
>
> (p. 178)

The temptation to celebrate and endorse human identities that are advantageous and then keep human identities that are disadvantageous silent arises for human beings when they are constructing their identities because 'a sense of identity can be a source not merely of pride and joy, but also of strength and confidence' (Sen, 2007, p. 1). A sense of identity can be a positive thing in that having a sense of identity is capable of making vital

> contribution to the strength and the warmth of our relations with others, such as neighbors, or members of the same community, or fellow citizens, or followers of the same religion. Our focus on particular identities can enrich our bonds and make us do many things for each other and can help to take us beyond our self-centered lives.
>
> (p. 2)

Having a sense of identity is not always positive; sometimes it is positive, sometimes it is negative, and at other times it is neither negative nor positive, but neutral (Abumere, 2023). The possibility of a sense of identity to be either positive, negative or neutral is attributable to the fact that: Firstly, 'the adversity of exclusion can be made to go hand in hand with the gifts of inclusion' (Sen, 2007, pp. 2–3); secondly, when exclusion and inclusion go *pari passu*, 'a sense of identity can firmly exclude many people even as it warmly embraces others' (p. 3).

The neutrality of a sense of identity is not what is at stake in the metaphysical empire debate. If colonial identity were perceived to be neutral by cultural appropriationists and mutual exclusivists, neither the former nor the latter will have any incentive to engage in the metaphysical empire debate. If cultural appropriationists perceived colonial identity to be neutral, they would probably not bother to accept it and argue for its appropriation; consequently there would probably be no cultural appropriationists in the first place. So too if mutual exclusivists perceived colonial identity to be neutral, they would probably not reject it and oppose its appropriation; consequently there would probably be no mutual exclusivists in the first place.

In the metaphysical empire debate, what is at stake is the positivity and negativity of identity. On the one hand, cultural appropriationists think that colonial identity is positive; for this reason, they are incentivised to accept it, and for the same reason they argue for its appropriation. On the other hand, mutual exclusivists think that colonial identity is negative; for this reason, they are incentivised to reject it, and for the same reason they oppose its appropriation.

Mutual exclusivists' concern about the negativity of colonial identity can be extended to identity in general. If we look

> around the world both historically and presently, we [will] see times and places when and where identity has been a source or even the source of negativities such as wars, discrimination, domination and other atrocities and violations and the consequent suffering and dehumanisation of the victims in the hands of the perpetrators.
>
> (Abumere, 2022, s.p.)

After all, Amartya Sen (2007), who through his theorisation and practical experience – and one may add from both *a priori* and *a posteriori* – knows what exactly having a negative sense of identity can do to us, says that

> identity can also kill – and kill with abandon. A strong – and exclusive – sense of belonging to one group can in many cases carry with it the perception of distance and divergence from other groups. Within-group solidarity can help to feed between-group discord.
>
> (p. 2)

Given the problem with having a negative sense of identity, Sen (2007) poses a rhetorical but important question: 'If identity-based thinking can be amenable to such brutal manipulation, where can the remedy be found?' (p. 3). Answering his own rhetorical question, he asserts that the solution to identity-based thinking's amenability to brutal manipulation

> can hardly be sought in trying to suppress or stifle the invoking of identity in general. For one thing, identity can be a source of richness and warmth as well as of violence and terror, and it would make little sense to treat identity as a general evil. Rather, we have to draw on the understanding that the force of a bellicose identity can be challenged by the power of competing identities. These can, of course, include the broad commonality of our shared humanity, but also many other identities that everyone simultaneously has. This leads to other ways of classifying people, which can restrain the exploitation of a specifically aggressive use of one particular categorisation.
>
> (pp. 3–4)

Looking at the African continent, it is apparent that what Sen refers to as the brutal manipulation of identity-based thinking is not only a historical phenomenon in Africa, but also a current phenomenon. The fact that it is simultaneously historical and current makes it even more alarming than if it were only historical or only current. Being simultaneously historical and current demonstrates that the legacies of identity puzzle endure on the continent and identity puzzle has been, and is still, an intractable problem on the continent.

No one can predict with mathematical certainty what exactly the future of identity puzzle will be on the continent, and we cannot claim any ability to predict with mathematical certainty what the future of identity puzzle will be on the continent. Even in physical and natural sciences and mathematics, room is given for margin of error when making predictions or forecast. But we cannot even predict or forecast the future of identity puzzle on the continent with margin of error. So, all we can do is to make an educated guess about the future of identity puzzle on the continent.

Nevertheless, even such an educated guess will still be a conjecture rather than a Gettierean knowledge in epistemological sense, that is, a justified true belief that is certain (Gettier, 1963).

The remit of this book is philosophical theorisation on identity, not scientific experiment on identity. So, without claiming any ability to make any prediction about the future of identity puzzle on the continent with mathematical certainty even with margin of error, I can only make an educated guess about the future of identity puzzle on the continent. In my educated guess, I think that if we look at the trajectory of identity puzzle on the continent from the past through the present to the future, we will see that:

> Alarmingly, the trajectory of the manipulation of identity-based thinking on the continent shows that the future (at least the near future) is certain (or at least highly probable) to converge with the past and the present. Whether in Central Africa (for example, Democratic Republic of Congo – DRC – and Cameroun), West Africa (for example, Nigeria and Mali), East Africa (for example, Kenya and Uganda), Southern Africa (for example, South Africa and Zimbabwe) or North Africa (for example, Libya and Egypt), the brutal manipulation of identity-based thinking pervades the continent.
>
> (Abumere, 2022, s.p.)

The brutal manipulation of identity-based thinking has not only engendered intra-state crises, but 'it has actually enabled tragic crises and conflicts in the past' (Abumere 2020, p. 351) at the inter-state level.

> The crises and conflicts manifested as early as the 1960s in East Africa and North Africa, and later in the 1970s in West Africa and Central Africa. For instance, in East Africa, after the war of independence between the Ethiopian government and Eritrean separatists from 1961 to 1991, Ethiopia and Eritrea fought a border war from 1998 to 2000, and engaged in a standoff from 2000 to 2018. While in confrontation with Ethiopia, Eritrea also had a border conflict with Djibouti in 2008 .... While in confrontation with Eritrea, Ethiopia fought a border war with Somalia from 1977 to 1978 over the ownership of the region of Ogaden.
>
> (p. 351)

Somalia too – following the pattern of Ethiopia and Eritrea – simultaneously engaged in two conflicts. At the time it was involved in a dispute with Ethiopia, it was also fighting a border war with Kenya from 1963 to 1967 in order to reclaim 'its lost territories including the Northern frontier district of Kenya' (Aremu, 2010, p. 550). Not to be left out in the East African conflicts, 'Tanzania and Uganda fought a border war over the Kagera Salient from 1978 to 1979. Prior to the war, political disagreements between

Kenya, Tanzania and Uganda led to the collapse of the EAC in 1977' (Abumere 2020, p. 351).

One can confidently argue that

> since colonialism is responsible for the geographical divisions and differences that are responsible for these wars, colonialism is (at least indirectly) responsible for the crises and conflicts. Ultimately, colonialism and the artificial separation of the peoples in these regions bear responsibility for the crises and conflicts.
>
> (Abumere, 2020, p. 351)

For this reason, those who are wary of the metaphysical empire think that since the metaphysical empire is ongoing-colonialism, the agenda of both the physical empire and the metaphysical empire is essentially the same and that, although the empires differ in form, they are similar in substance. While the physical empire was brute and coercive in its modus operandi, the metaphysical empire is insidious in its modus operandi.

For those who are wary of the metaphysical empire because it is perceived as the perpetuation of the physical and geographical empire in other ways, that is, the continuation of colonialisation by other means, the aforementioned crises and conflicts – which resulted from the brutal manipulation of identity-based thinking – are a function of the physical and geographical empire which simultaneously engineered both the identities that were manipulated and engendered the manipulation of the identities. Valentin Y. Mudimbe (2003)'s assertion that 'the predicament of African identities … was in actuality engineered by the colonial library' (p. 212) corroborates the aforementioned claim. This is not surprising because Africans had, and continue to have, almost the same experience in terms of European and White imperial, colonial, neocolonial and racist marginalisation; discrimination and domination whether in the cultural, social, political or economic sphere (Ndlovu-Gatsheni & Mhlanga, 2013).

The onus is on Africans in general and African thinkers in particular to rectify the vicious 'manipulation of identity-based thinking because, among other factors such as co-existence on the same continent, political, economic and so on' (Abumere, 2023, p. 16), it is the morally right thing to do both deontologically and consequentially. After all, we will always have to live with strangers, whether we are the strangers in their land or they are the strangers in our land. It is normal that among a group of people, at least some of them, if not many of them, and in their lifetimes, at least sometimes if not many times, will have to live as strangers in a land or place that is not theirs or that is not originally theirs (see Ndlovu-Gatsheni & Mhlanga, 2013). When such strangers live long enough in such land or place, it may become their land or place too and they may call it home.

This assertion about some of us being strangers sometimes in our lifetimes is not only true in contemporary times; it is also true in historical times. The renown African historian Toyin Falola (2006) was apt to note that 'Africans have always been on the move, ever since the time they created civilisation and scattered it around the continent and elsewhere' (p. 1). After all, it is indisputable that, as Willard (1970) says, 'the interpenetration of so many different foreign cultures with so many varying indigenous ones makes culture clash a problem for every … African state' (p. vii). Consequently, that is in view of this interpenetration and culture clash, 'when commenting on the predicament of African identities, without rejecting the realities of such identities' (Abumere, 2023, p. 16), we ought to discard identity-based thinking that is not accommodative of identities that are not ours. It is for this reason that Mudimbe (2003) admonishes us to be wary of 'the potential dangers of perspectives that in the name of difference would value as essences what was in actuality engineered by the colonial library' (p. 212).

Bibliography

Abumere, F. A. (2015) *Different Perspectives on Global Justice: A Fusion of Horizons*. Bielefeld, Publication at Bielefeld University.

Abumere, F. A. (2019) Rule of law. In: Romaniuk, S., Thapa, M. & Marton, P. (eds.) *The Palgrave Encyclopedia of Global Security Studies*. Cham, Palgrave Macmillan, s.p.

Abumere, F. A. (2020) Introducing normativity in African international politics. *Politikon: South African Journal of Political Studies* 47 (3), 342–360.

Abumere, F. A. (2022) *Normativity in African Regional Relations*. London, Rowman & Littlefield.

Abumere, F. A. (2023) *African Identities and International Politics*. London, Routledge.

Achebe, C. (1982) Interview with Anthony Appiah, D. A. N. Jones and John Ryle. *Times Literary Supplement*, February 26.

Adair, M. & Powell, S. (1988) *The Subjective Side of Politics*. San Francisco, CA, Tools for Change.

Andreasen, R. O. (1998) A new perspective on the race debate. *British Journal for the Philosophy of Science* 49 (2), 199–225.

Appiah, K. A. (1992) *In My Father's House: Africa in the Philosophy of Culture*. Oxford, Oxford University Press.

Appiah, K. A. (1996) Race, culture, identity: Misunderstood connections. In: Appiah, K. A. & Gutmann, A. (eds.) *Colour Conscious: The Political Morality of Race*. Princeton, NJ, Princeton University Press, pp. 30–105.

Aremu, J. O. (2010) Conflicts in Africa: Meaning, causes, impact and solution. *African Research Review* 4 (4), 549–560.

Berenskoetter, F. (2017) Identity in international relations. In: Sandal, N. (ed.) *Oxford Research Encyclopedias, International Studies*, December, s.p. Oxford, Oxford University Press.

Blum, L. (2002). *"I'm Not a Racist, But ...": The Moral Quandary of Race*. Ithaca, NY, Cornell University Press.
Bray, Z. (2008) Ethnographic approaches. In: della Porta, D. & Keating, K. (eds.) *Approaches and Methodologies in the Social Sciences: A Pluralist Perspective*. Cambridge, Cambridge University Press, pp. 296–315.
Brubaker, R. & Cooper, F. (2000). Beyond "identity". *Theory and Society* 29, 1–47.
Burke, A. (2006). Identity/difference. In: Griffiths, M. (ed.) *Encyclopedia of International Relations and Global Politics*. London, Routledge, 394–396.
Campbell, D. (1992) *Writing Security: United States Foreign Policy and the Politics of Identity*. Manchester, Manchester University Press.
Chisom, R. & Washington, M. (1997). *Undoing Racism: A Philosophy of International Social Change*, 2nd ed. New Orleans, LA, The People's Institute Press.
Cronin, B. (1999) *Community under Anarchy: Transnational Identity and the Evolution of Cooperation*. New York, Columbia University Press.
Falola, T. (2006) *Welcome. Conference Program, Movements, Migrations, and Displacements in Africa, Africa Conference*, The University of Texas at Austin, Austin, TX, March 25–27.
Fanon, F. (1967). *Black Skin, White Mask*. London, Grove Press.
Gadamer, H-G. (1989). *Truth and Method*. New York, Crossroad.
Gallie, W. B. (1956) Essentially contested concepts. *Proceedings of the Aristotelian Society* 56, 167–198.
Gettier, E. L. (1963) Is justified true belief knowledge? *Analysis* 23 (6), 121–123.
Goldberg, D. T. (1993) *Racist Culture: Philosophy and the Politics of Meaning*. Oxford, Blackwell.
Gyekye, K. (1995) *An Essay on African Philosophical Thought: The Akan Conceptual Scheme*. Philadelphia, PA, Temple University Press.
Harris, V. & Ordoña, T. (1990) Developing unity among women of colour: Crossing the barriers of internalized racism and cross racial hostility. In: Anzaldúa, G. (ed.) *Making Face, Making Soul: Hacienda Caras*. San Francisco, CA, Aunt Lute Press, pp. 304–316.
Haslanger, S. (2000). Gender and race: (What) are they? (what) do we want them to be? *Noûs* 34 (1), 31–55.
Heyes, C. J. (2020) Identity politics. *The Stanford Encyclopedia of Philosophy*, Fall ed. http://plato.stanford.edu/archives/fall2020/entries/identitypolitics/
Hopf, T. (1998) The promise of constructivism in international relations theory. *International Security* 23, 171–200.
Kitcher, P. (1999) Race, ethnicity, biology, culture. In: Harris. L. (ed.) *Racism*. Amherst, NY, Humanity Books, pp. 87–117.
Kitcher, P. (2007) Does "race" have a future? *Philosophy and Public Affairs* 35 (4), 293–317.
Lawrence, K. & Keleher, T. (2004) *Race and Public Policy Conference*, Aspen Institute Round Table on Community Change, The Aspen Institute, Washington, D.C., June.

Macintosh, P. (1989). Unpacking the invisible knapsack. Working paper #189 White privilege and male privilege: A personal account of coming to see correspondences through work in women's studies. Wellesley College Center for the Study of Women, Wellesley, MA.

Mafeje, A. (2008 [2000]) Africanity: A combative ontology. *CODESRIA Bulletin* 3rd & 4th, 106–110.

Mbembe, A. (2002) African modes of self-writing. *Public Culture* 14 (1), 239–273.

Mbembe, A. (2019) Thoughts on the planetary: An interview with Achille Mbembe. In: Bangstad, S. & Torbjorn, T. N. (eds.) *New Frame*, September 5. https://www.newframe.com/thoughts-on-the-planetary-an-interview-with-achille-mbembe/

Mills, C. W. (1998). *Blackness Visible: Essays on Philosophy and Race*. Ithaca, NY, Cornell University Press.

Mudimbe, V. Y. (2003) Globalization and African identity. *CR: The New Centennial Review* 3 (2), 205–218.

Ndlovu-Gatsheni, S. J. (2018) Metaphysical empire, linguicide and cultural imperialism. *English Academy Review* 35 (2), 96–115.

Ndlovu-Gatsheni, S. J. & Mhlanga, B. (2013) Introduction. In: Ndlovu-Gatsheni, S. J. & Mhlanga, B. (eds.) *Bondage of Boundaries and Identity Politics in Postcolonial Africa: The Northern Problem and Ethno-Futures*. Pretoria, Africa Institute of South Africa, 1–22.

Sen, A. (2007) *Identity and Violence: The Illusion of Violence*. New York, W.W. Norton.

Shelby, T. (2012) Race. In: Estlund, D. (ed.) *The Oxford Handbook of Political Philosophy*. Oxford, Oxford University Press, pp. 336–353.

Sundstrom, R. (2002) "Racial" nominalism. *Journal of Social Philosophy* 33 (2): 193–210.

Taylor, P. C. (2004) *Race: A Philosophical Introduction*. Cambridge, Polity Press.

Vessey, D. (n.d.) Gadamer and the fusion of horizons. https://www.davevessey.com/gadamer_Horizons.htm

Wa Thiong'o, N. (2013) Resisting metaphysical empires: Language as a war zone. *The Third John La Rose Memorial Lecture*, Senate House, University of London, London, October 2.

Wa Thiong'o, N. (2014) *Resisting Metaphysical Empires: Language as a War Zone*. London, New Beacon Books.

Willard, J. (1970) *Cameroon Federation: Political Integration in a Fragmentary Society*. Princeton, NJ, Princeton University Press.

Wiredu, K. (1997) *Cultural Universals and Particulars: An African Perspective*. Bloomington, IN, Indiana University Press.

Wiredu, K. & Gyekye, K. (1992) *Person and Community: Ghanaian Philosophical Studies*. Washington, D.C., The Council of Research in Values and Philosophy.

Zack, N. (2002) *Philosophy of Science and Race*. New York, Routledge.

4 Universals versus Particulars

Humanity versus Identity

Identity and the Value Placed on It

In the discussion in the preceding chapter, I focused on the conceptual and theoretical framework of the book, which revolves around the phenomenon of identity. In the preceding chapter, I dealt with the question of race and the problem of identity. I started by briefly teasing out the concept of race. After the discussion on race, I explained the concept of identity, the kind of identity I am concerned about and how this in turn informs the value that mutual exclusivists place on racial identity. Then, I explained that the preliminary discussion on race and identity in the preceding chapter will be explored in detail in the subsequent chapters, which include the current chapter.

In the preceding chapter, I introduced and explicated the phenomenon of identity in both its narrow sense (racial identity) and broad sense in order to prepare the grounds for the discussion in the remainder of the book. Based on the preliminary discussion of the phenomenon of identity in the preceding chapter, I will engage in a detailed analysis of the implications of this phenomenon for the debate on the metaphysical empire in this chapter and in the remainder of this book. So, beginning with this chapter, I shall explore (albeit indirectly rather than directly or implicitly rather than explicitly) the impact of race and identity on the metaphysical empire debate. This I will do by exploring the cultural universals versus cultural particulars debate.

Since racial identity in particular and identity in general are the principal determinants of where Africans stand on the question of the metaphysical empire and the decolonisation debate, it was important that I explained my conception of both the concept of race and the concept of identity. That explanation was the subject matter of the preceding chapter. Just as I did in the preceding chapter, in this chapter I shall continue my explanation of why and how the concepts of race and identity play key roles in the enduring legacies of colonialism which are simultaneously manifested and reflected in *ongoing-colonialism*, that is, a combination of

DOI: 10.4324/9781003589839-4

colonialism, neocolonialism and the metaphysical empire. However, while I directly or explicitly engaged the question of race and the problem of identity in the preceding chapter, I will only indirectly or implicitly deal with race and identity in this chapter. In other words, while the focus of the preceding chapter was race and identity, the focus of this chapter is not race and identity as such.

In view of the discussion on identity in the preceding chapter, I agree with Johnson Willard (1970) that

> identity is a matter of the significance of a thing, a question of purpose and perspective. The achievement of a sense of identity is most significant when it involves acquiring a sense of oneness from many separate distinct events or objects, when it is a question of parts and wholes. (p. 6)

Based on this conception of identity, I think that one can plausibly argue that individuals and collectives value identity. Put differently, as far as individuals and collectives are concerned, identity is a valuable possession.

To understand what makes identity valuable and how valuable identity is, Steven Mintz (2018)'s two conceptions of value are helpful. In the first instance, he conceives of value in a narrow sense, while in the second instance he conceives of value in a broad sense. On the one hand, value (in the singular), narrowly construed *a la* Mintz (2018), 'is that which is good, desirable, or worthwhile' (s.p.). On the other hand, values (in the plural), broadly construed *a la* Mintz (2018):

> are basic and fundamental beliefs that guide or motivate attitudes or actions. They help us to determine what is important to us. Values describe the personal qualities we choose to embody to guide our actions; the sort of person we want to be; the manner in which we treat ourselves and others, and our interaction with the world around us. They provide the general guidelines for conduct …. Values are the motive behind purposeful action. They are the ends to which we act. (s.p.)

In line with Mintz's narrow conception of value, identity is valuable because it is good, desirable or worthwhile. While in line with Mintz's broad conception of value, identity is valuable because it is a basic belief which we have and which regulates our behaviour. In this sense, identity determines what we consider to be significant and it determines our character, how we perceive ourselves and others, and how we relate to ourselves and others, both those we share the same identity with and those we do not share the same identity with.

In the metaphysical empire debate, what exactly separates cultural appropriationists from mutual exclusivists is the kind of value both sides place on identity. Both sides value identity; however, they value identity in different ways. While cultural appropriationists think that since culture is dynamic, colonial linguistic appropriation does not in any way dilute the African identity, mutual exclusivists think that the only way to have authentic cultures in Africa is to discard colonial heritage such as European languages and return to or remain with original African cultures and languages.

Having explained what the metaphysical empire is in the introductory chapter, having resolved the quandary between cultural appropriationism and mutual exclusivism in the penultimate chapter, and having discussed race and identity in the preceding chapter, in this current chapter – taking a cue from Kwasi Wiredu (1997)'s reflection on cultural universals and cultural particulars – I shall draw insights from metaphysics to simultaneously delineate the (metaphorical) boundaries of the metaphysical empire and tease out the grounds on which African cultures can appropriate some useful aspects of Western cultures without the danger of falling into the metaphysical empire.

In his endeavour to reconcile cultural particulars with cultural universals, Wiredu asserts that there is

> a universal characteristic by which all human beings, regardless of their particularities, are human beings. It is the case that all human beings communicate and that communication is grounded in a shared human biology. Despite the enormous difficulties of intercultural exchange, communication is, at least in principle, always possible.
> (Wirth, 2000, p. 158)

Wiredu (1997) does not deny the fact that there are disparities in cultures. However, in his words, 'the fundamental biological similarity of all human beings assures the possibility of resolving all such disparities, for the foundation of communication is biological' (p. 20). Basing his argument on biology and admitting the possible limitation of the biological argument, Wiredu (1996) says that even though on the one hand 'there is the notion of an advance beyond the biological at the human level', on the other hand 'there is no suggestion of an ontological transcendence of the biological' (p. 36).

Given that intuition is innate rather than acquired, it is a noticeable, or at least a possible, piece of evidence in support of his assertion that 'there is no suggestion of an ontological transcendence of the biological' (Wiredu, 1996, p. 36). In philosophy, intuition refers to the capacity to obtain

> knowledge that cannot be acquired either by inference or observation, by reason or experience. As such, intuition is thought of as an original, independent source of knowledge, since it is designed to account for just those kinds of knowledge that other sources do not provide. Knowledge of necessary truths and of moral principles is sometimes explained in this way.
>
> (The Editors, 2024, s.p.)

Considering intuition as a cultural universal, Henry Odera Oruka (1990) says intuition is a 'form of mental skill which helps the mind to extrapolate from experience and come to establish extra statistical inductive truths – or to make a correct/plausible logical inference without any established or known rules of procedures' (p. 29). Since intuition is innate rather than acquired, it is safe to say that it is biological. If it is biological, then it is safe to say that Wiredu is right that we, as human beings, have not ontologically transcended the biological. And if both Africans and Westerners share common human biology, then it is possible for the former and the latter to have inter-cultural communication.

I am not really interested in, or I am less interested in, using biology and biological arguments in the metaphysical empire debate. I am interested in, or more interested in, using pure philosophical arguments in the metaphysical empire debate. Nevertheless, I find Wiredu's biological arguments to be convincing and I find the way he uses biological arguments to support philosophical arguments to be interesting. It is this combination of biology and philosophy that enables him to reach the kind of conclusion he reaches. And I agree with his conclusion. Like Wiredu (1997), I think that 'universals, rightly conceived on the basis of our common biological identity, are not incompatible with cultural particularities and, in fact, are what make intercultural communication possible' (s.p.).[1]

Like Wiredu (1997), I shall 'confront the paradox that while Western cultures recoil from claims of universality, previously colonised peoples, seeking to redefine their identities, insist on cultural particularities' (s.p.).[2] The discussion on how to find the right 'models of cultural exchange between Africa and her former colonisers has often dominated the recent practice of African philosophy' (Wirth, 2000, p. 157). So, it is not something that Wiredu invented or began. However, what makes his contribution to the discussion innovative and seminal is that he

> centres this discussion on the relationship between universalisable truths and norms (ideas and values that hold for all peoples in all cultures) and the particularity of truths and norms (ideas and values that hold for a specific culture and/or time period).
>
> (Wirth, 2000, p. 157)

Following in the footsteps of Wiredu is helpful for my endeavour to reconcile mutual exclusivism with cultural appropriationism because the disagreement between mutual exclusivists and cultural appropriationists in the metaphysical empire debate is in some ways similar to the disagreement on cultural particulars and cultural universals in metaphysics, and I think Wiredu has succeeded in reconciling, or at least he has attempted to reconcile, cultural particulars and cultural universals.

Based on experience drawn from his communitarian Akan culture and philosophical knowledge gained as an academic philosopher, Wiredu navigates, or at least 'attempts to navigate a middle path between a hard doctrine of universals and a hare doctrine of relativism' (Wirth, 2000 pp. 157–158). Therefore, in the next sub-chapter, I shall explore and engage Wiredu's seminal philosophisation on the relationship between cultural universals and cultural particulars.

Cultural Universals versus Cultural Particulars

If the Nigerian philosopher Kolawole Owolabi (1999) is right, and I think he is, that 'a prominent issue that has dominated the enterprise of African philosophy since its inception in the written form is the question of how to define African identity' (p. 22), then identity has the value I said it has in the preceding chapter and the preceding sub-chapter. As another Nigerian philosopher Fayemi (2011) says, and I think he too is right,

> most intellectual discussions in African philosophy are reactions to this problem of identity. Two things are largely responsible for this search for African identity. One is the negative impact of the colonial experience of domination and exploitation in Africa. The second is the ethnocentric assertion of Western scholarship to the denigration of anything that is African.
>
> (p. 259)

Over three decades ago, Owolabi (1999) informs us that there are two prevailing schools of thought in the search of African self-identity and African self-conception. One of the prevailing schools of thought begins by believing and acknowledging – rightly or wrongly – that Western philosophy in particular and Western thought in general are culturally pluralistic. Then this school of thought goes on to argue that Western culture is not superior to African culture or any other culture for that matter. For this school of thought, no one culture is superior to another culture and there is no such thing as hierarchy when cultures are concerned (p. 24).

Based on their argument that the African culture is not inferior to any non-African culture, African philosophers and thinkers who are champions of the aforementioned school of thought[3] set out to discover a distinctive and authentic African identity by arguing that there are things that each culture has which cannot be inter-culturally communicated with another culture or other cultures. In other words, they believe in cultural particulars, they think that there are cultural particulars, and they argue for cultural particulars. In their endeavour to discover a distinctive and authentic African identity, since they believe in cultural particulars, they concentrate their effort on discovering especially the cultural particulars of the African culture that were hitherto unappreciated and ignored (p. 24).

The aforementioned school of thought has had different champions at different epochs, all of them in the second half of the twentieth century. In the 1950s, especially in the late 1950s, it was famously championed by Placide Temples (1959). In the 1960s, by Abraham and famously by John Mbiti – Abraham (1966) in the mid-1960s and Mbiti (1969) in the late 1960s. Sodipo (1975) in the 1970s, especially in the mid-1970s. Anyanwu (1983) in the 1980s, especially in the early 1980s. And famously Leopold Sedar Senghor (1991) in the 1990s, especially in the early 1990s. One thing, among others, that all of them have in common is that they are sanguine that they can prove that the African culture has particularities or distinctiveness which no other culture has. Therefore, they champion an African philosophy that stresses the distinctiveness of the African culture (Owolabi, 1999, p. 24).

As far as the aforementioned champions of the first prevailing school of thought are concerned – from ethno-philosophers such as Temples and Mbiti, to cultural nationalists and leaders of negritude such as Senghor – 'all philosophies are cultural philosophies and no philosophical datum of any given culture is applicable to other cultures' (p. 24). For this reason, it will not be far-fetched to say that, and I think we can deduce that, in the metaphysical empire debate, they would support mutual exclusivism and oppose cultural appropriationism.

The second prevailing school of thought is not sanguine that we can prove that the African culture, or any culture for that matter, has its own particularities or distinctiveness. Therefore, in view of the problem of African identity and African self-conception in African philosophy in particular and African thought in general, this school of thought rejects the Western anthropological depiction, or more accurately caricature, of Africa as a cultural relativistic and ethnocentric place (p. 24).

Champions of the second school of thought admit that some aspects of cultures vary from society to society. However, they argue that in spite of the fact that each society has some cultural practices that are peculiar, 'human cultures still share certain fundamental traits that allow for cross-cultural comparisons and interactions' (p. 24). For this reason, African philosophers who are champions of the school of thought think that it is possible to have inter-cultural communication between the African culture and non-African cultures.

In the twentieth century, between the 1980s and the 1990s – Wiredu (1980) and Paulin Hountondji (1983) in the early 1980s, Peter Bodunrin (1985) in the mid-1980s, and Towa (1991) and Kwame Anthony Appiah (1992) – champions of the aforementioned school of thought maintained that there are cultural universals and they were sanguine that they would be able to prove the existence of cultural universals and the possibility of inter-cultural communication between the African culture and non-African cultures (Fayemi, 2011, p. 260). For this reason, it will not be far-fetched to say that, and I think we can deduce that, in the metaphysical empire debate, they would support cultural appropriationism and oppose mutual exclusivism.

Looking at the disagreement between the two prevailing schools of thought, we see that there is no canonical agreement on what exactly the African identity is, or what exactly the African self-conception ought to be. Consequently, there is no agreement on what exactly the African culture is – is it static and devoid of foreign influences or is it dynamic and receptive of the integration of certain aspects of other cultures? What is self-evident in, or at least what we can infer from, the disagreement between the first prevailing school of thought and the second prevailing school of thought is that as far as the problem of African identity is concerned, and as far as the question of African self-conception is concerned, there is a contrast and incongruity between what some African philosophers and thinkers such as Temples, Abraham, Mbiti, Sodipo, Anyanwu and Senghor think and what other African philosophers such as Wiredu, Hountondji, Bodunrin, Towa and Appiah think (Fayemi, 2011, p. 260).

The disagreement between mutual exclusivists and cultural appropriationists in the metaphysical empire debate is a derivative of the disagreement between the aforementioned first prevailing school of thought and the aforementioned second prevailing school of thought. If we acknowledge cultural universals and accept the possibility of inter-cultural communication between the African culture and Western culture, then we will accept cultural appropriation. And if we accept cultural appropriation, then we might not be too worried about the metaphysical empire. But if reject cultural universals and the possibility of inter-cultural communication between the African culture and Western culture, then we will reject cultural appropriation. And if we reject cultural appropriation, then we will have every reason to be very worried about the metaphysical empire.

It was probably in view of the aforementioned disagreements that someone like Aime Cesaire absolutely rejected provincialism when he categorically stated that 'I'm not going to confine myself to some narrow particularism. Nor do I intend to lose myself in a disembodied universalism' (qtd. in Grosfoguel, 2011, p. 1). According to Cesaire,

> there are two ways to lose oneself: through walled-in segregation in the particular, or through dissolution into the 'universal.' My idea of the universal is that of a universal with all that is particular, rich with all particulars, the deepening and coexistence of all particulars.
>
> (qtd. in Grosfoguel, 2011, p. 1)

On African culture in general and African identity or African self-conception in particular, in spite of the aforementioned disagreement between the first prevailing school of thought and the second prevailing school of thought, and between mutual exclusivists and cultural appropriationists, we can still decipher whether the African culture is receptive of cultural appropriation or not. One way of doing the deciphering is to look at the social character of African ethics and see how it enjoins us to relate with fellow humans whether they are members of our society or not, or whether they are Africans or not.

Kwame Gyekye (2011) argues that humanism is the foundation of African ethics (sect. 10). Humanism is understood as 'the doctrine that considers human interests and welfare as basic to the thought and action of the people' (sect. 10). He argues that this conception of humanism in African ethics is what engendered communitarianism in African societies is. Then he argues that in view of the social character of African ethics and the communitarian nature of African societies, it is almost impossible for the needs of members of an African community to be met outside the community (sect. 10).

Furthermore, he says that

> the communitarian ethos is also borne of beliefs about the natural sociality of the human being, expressed, for instance, in the Akan maxim … that says that 'when a human being descends from the heavens, he descends into a human town' (*onipa firi soro besi a, obesi onipa kurom*).
>
> (sect. 10) (emphasis in original)

Consequently, for him,

> social or community life is … not optional to the human being. Social life, which follows upon our natural sociality, implicates the individual in a web of moral obligations, commitments, and duties to be fulfilled in pursuit of the common good or the general welfare.
>
> (sect. 10)

In view of the above, Gyekye (2011) argues that African humanitarian ethics is derived from

> social morality, the morality of the common good, and the morality of duty that is so comprehensive as to bring within its compass what are referred to as moral ideals (such as love, virtue, compassion), which are considered supererogatory in Western ethics.
>
> (sect. 10)

Because of the emphasis on moral ideals, character is essential in African ethics,

> for the success of the moral life is held to be a function of the quality of an individual's personal life. A moral conception of personhood is held in African ethics, the conception that there are certain basic moral norms and ideals to which the conduct of the individual human being, if he is a person, ought to conform.
>
> (sect. 10)

In the context of the metaphysical empire debate, the most striking thing about the humanistic nature and social character of African ethics is that African ethics recognises 'all human beings as brothers by reason of our common humanity' (sect. 10). For Gyekye (2011), such recognition is actually

> a lofty moral ideal that must be cherished and made a vital or robust feature of global ethics in our contemporary world. It is a bulwark against developing bigoted attitudes toward peoples of different cultures or skin colours who are, also, members of the universal human family called race.
>
> (sect. 10)

There is no doubt that someone like Wiredu is conscious of the aforementioned universal human family. More importantly, he values it. After all, in his work on cultural universals and cultural particulars, he does not only teach us 'some important lessons about the heterogeneity of languages'; he also teaches us some important lessons about 'the heterogeneity of human goodness' (Wirth, 2000, p. 159).

It is probably in view of the aforementioned universal human family that someone like Wiredu is insistent that cultural universals and cultural particulars are not mutually exclusive and that inter-cultural communication is indeed possible between cultures. In his influential work on cultural universals and particulars, he

> confronts the paradox that while Western cultures recoil from claims of universality, previously colonized peoples, seeking to redefine their identities, insist on cultural particularities. Wiredu

> asserts that universals, rightly conceived on the basis of our common biological identity, are not incompatible with cultural particularities and, in fact, are what make intercultural communication possible. Drawing on aspects of Akan thought that appear to diverge from Western conceptions in the areas of ethics and metaphysics, Wiredu calls for a just reappraisal of these disparities, free of thought patterns corrupted by a colonial mentality. Wiredu's exposition of the principles of African traditional philosophy is not purely theoretical; he shows how certain aspects of African political thought may be applied to the practical resolution of some of Africa's most pressing problems.
>
> (Wiredu, 1997, s.p.)[4]

Wiredu (1996) asks us to imagine that cultural universals did not exist. He says in such a scenario there will be no inter-cultural communication. Absent cultural universals, absent inter-cultural communication because cultural universals are a necessary and sufficient condition for inter-cultural communication. Following this logic, he says since there is inter-cultural communication, cultural universals exist (p. 21).

In defence of cultural universals, Wiredu (1996) argues that what it means, or at least part of what it means, to be human is to have more than instinct and predisposition to self-preservation. Humans are also, and importantly, thinking beings. In other words, by virtue of being human, we necessarily have 'more than instinct in the drive for equilibrium and self- preservation' (p. 23). Importantly, if not more important at least equally important, we are capable of 'reflective perception, abstraction, deduction and induction. In their basic nature, these mental capacities are the same for all humans; irrespective of whether they inhabit Europe, Asia or Africa' (Wiredu, 1996, p. 23).

Considering human nature and the biological constitution of the human person, Wiredu (1996) says that we can safely make a two-fold assumption about the human species. Firstly, we can safely assume that there are certain essential classifications and criteria of thought which the entire human kind shares in common (p. 45). In view of this safe assumption, Wiredu (1996) says that:

> The human constitution of flesh and bones, quickened by electrical charges and wrapped up in variously pigmented integument, is the same everywhere; while there is only one world in which we all live, move, and have our struggles, notwithstanding such things as the vagaries of climate. These fact, which underlie the possibility of communication among kith and kin, are the same facts that underlie the possibility of communication among the various peoples of the world.
>
> (p. 23)

Secondly, in spite of the classifications and criteria of thought which the entire human kind shares in common, there are certain profound differences among the different ethnicities or groups of the human race when it comes to their methods or ways of conceptualisation in certain delicate aspects of thought (p. 45). However, in spite of this second assumption and in view of the first assumption, Wiredu (1996) says that the fact that inter-cultural communication is possible means that the second assumption does not negate the first assumption. As he says,

> without communication, community is impossible, and without thought, communication is impossible. But without some common norms of talk, communication is impossible, and without common norms of thought, common norms of talk are unavoidable. Therefore, without some common norms of thought a human community is impossible.
>
> (p. 34)

A cursory reading, not even a careful reading, of Wiredu suggests that he thinks that the possibility of inter-cultural communication, the plausibility of the aforementioned first assumption, and the fact that the aforementioned second assumption does not negate the first assumption are not only supported by biology and metaphysics, they are also all supported by logic and ethics. His claim that even logic and ethics support his defence of cultural universals is not even implicit; it is explicit.

Let us first take a look at the logic claim and then take a look at the ethics claim. In terms of the logic claim, considering the logical principles of non-contradiction and induction, Wiredu (1996) avers that 'it is apparent that together they unite the human activities of understanding and knowing in such a way as to make it impossible that different peoples might be able to communicate but unable to argue rationally among themselves' (p. 24).

Concerning the ethics claim, Wiredu (1996) says our common morality is other-regarding, and as such, as ethical beings we are not merely self-interested, we are also other-interested in our thoughts and actions. So, a moral agent does not just act without contemplating the impact of her actions on others and their interests. When a moral agent acts, she contemplates the impact of her actions on others and their interests, and she imagines herself to be in their position – she puts herself in their shoes so to speak. Having imagined herself in their position or having put herself in their shoes, she is able to unselfishly comprehend the impact of her actions on them and their interests, and consequently, she is able to accept the impact in a way that it will change her actions which will in turn change the impact to be more accommodative of the interests of others (p. 30).

In spite of the fact that our common morality is other-regarding, 'inter-cultural communication often runs into the notoriously thorny problem of ethical relativism' (Wirth, 2000, p. 158). However, in spite of the fact that 'cultural exchange encounters heterogeneous normative practices, Wiredu finds it dangerous to conclude from this that there can be no impartial moral position to resolve competing moral claims' (p. 158). Therefore, he complements the moral principle of other-regarding with the moral principle of sympathetic impartiality. Wiredu (1997)'s sympathetic impartiality states that a human being or a moral agent has and demonstrates 'manifest due concern for the interest of others if in contemplating the impact of his actions on their interests, she puts herself imaginatively in their position, and having done so, is able to welcome the impact' (p. 29).

Taking his cue from Immanuel Kant's ethics, particularly his categorical imperative,

> Wiredu searches for a moral precept that is not the unjustifiable universalisation of a particular custom. He injects 'a dose of compassion' into Kant's stern formalism and derives a kinder and gentler categorical imperative that he calls 'sympathetic impartiality.' Dedicated to the 'harmonisation of interests in society,' this moral precept [is] akin to the Golden Rule.
>
> (Wirth, 2000, p. 158) (emphasis in original)

Remember that the Golden Rule says do to others what you would want them to do to you (and the Silver Rule says do not do to others what you would not want them to do to you). In the same spirit, the moral principle of sympathetic impartiality says do not act in such a way that the consequences of your actions will impact or affect people and their interests in the manner that you will not want you and your interests to be impacted or affected by other people's actions. It is simply for this Golden Rule reason that the precept, as mentioned earlier, states that the moral agent has to 'manifest due concern for the interest of others if in contemplating the impact of his actions on their interests, he puts himself imaginatively in their position, and having done so, is able to welcome the impact' (Wiredu, 1997, p. 29).

According to Wiredu (1996), the aforementioned moral principle of other-regarding, in combination with the moral principle of sympathetic impartiality, is 'a human universal transcending culture viewed as social forms and customary beliefs and practices. In being common to all human practice of morality; it is a universal of any non-brutish form of human life' (p. 31). However, Henry Odera Oruka (1990) argues that

> individuals lack sympathetic impartiality and they do not even acquire it in a civil state otherwise there would be little need for police, prisons and class wars. They remain egoists and many of them are still rational, otherwise the society would have melted away.
>
> (p. 27)

In spite of Oruka's disagreement with Wiredu on sympathetic impartiality, the moral principles of other-regarding and sympathetic impartiality are some of the pillars of the social grounds for Wiredu's defence of cultural universals. The social grounds for Wiredu's defence of cultural universals is very important because as D. A. Masolo (2005) says:

> Wiredu contributes and adds an African tone to the familiar and perhaps one of the most influential preoccupations of twentieth-century philosophy, viz., analytic theories on the relation between language, meaning, and mind. What he adds to the literature is the view that meaning cannot be understood in pure logical terms without the collective and relational social base that makes the very idea of meaning possible. Meanings and, by implication, mind, are objective in the sense that they are biologically made possible, and not in the sense that they exist as entities independently of the communicative act.
>
> (par. 27)

In spite of the social grounds mentioned earlier, and in spite of the defences that are based on biology, metaphysics, logic and ethics, Wiredu does not think that cultural universals trump cultural particulars. Obviously he does not also think that cultural particulars trump cultural universals. His endeavour is the balancing of the former and the latter. Just as I argue for 'qualified' decolonisation rather than an 'unqualified' decolonisation, decolonisation with a caveat rather than decolonisation without a caveat, or accommodative decolonisation rather than a non-accommodative decolonisation, so too Wiredu argues for moderate expression of cultural universals and cultural particulars rather than an absolute expression of one which negates the other. As he says, as human beings, we can neither live by cultural universals alone nor live by cultural particulars alone. As human beings, we need a combination of both the former and the latter in order to live (Wiredu, 1997, p. 9).

What I have learned from Wiredu, and I think what mutual exclusivists and cultural appropriationists can learn from Wiredu, is the balancing of cultural universals and cultural particulars. The lesson I learned from Wiredu on the balancing of cultural universals and cultural particulars is the reason I am sanguine that mutual exclusivism and cultural appropriationism can be synthesised in order to arrive at an accommodative decolonisation. Anyone can easily learn this lesson by realising that just as cultural universals and cultural particulars are not mutually exclusive, so too in the context of the metaphysical empire debate, the views of mutual exclusivists and the views of cultural appropriationists are not mutually exclusive.

However, as expected, there are people who disagree with Wiredu's views on the existence of cultural universals or the relationship between cultural universals and cultural particulars. Even when some agree with him that he is right about the existence of cultural universals, they think he is wrong about the relationship between cultural universals and cultural particulars. Some even think that he misconstrues cultural universals with cultural particulars, while others think that the distinction between cultural universals and cultural particulars is superfluous; hence, the discussion on, and the reconciliation of, cultural universals and cultural particulars is a project in futility.

Bello (2004) says that 'it is neither necessary nor important to classify problems, data, ideas, concepts or techniques as either universal or particular, especially since Wiredu himself concedes that the universality of a mode of conceptualisation does not guarantee its objective validity' (p. 267). Consequently, Bello (2004) advises us not to restrict 'our thoughts to ideas we reckon universals, for whatever reason[s], whether linguistic or indigent of language' (p. 267). And Keita (1997) says that 'Wiredu is correct in arguing that there are cultural universals, but they are none other than the general forms of what we refer to as cultural particulars' (p. 134).

In spite of rebuttals such as Keita's and Bello's, Wiredu (2002) remains sanguine that although people belong to different cultures, as they

> interact more and more and become more and more familiar with each other's languages and philosophies, with any fallacies of racial superiority dropped, one can expect that there will be increasing cross-appropriation, and consequently, cross-fertilisation of ideas; so that cultural difference will become more and more unreliable as an index to philosophical difference.
>
> (p. 204)

However, focusing on language, Barry Hallen (1995) argues that:

> While the assumption of the universality of meaning that enables cross-cultural linguistic interaction possesses obvious utility for a field linguist, who is confronted with the need to translate an alien language, the resultant manual if translated cannot preclude an ethnocentric bias, since the translator will likely favour the meaning of their own native language – English, for example, effectively universalizing them into propositions, and then proceed to impose English meanings upon other languages via the process of translation.
>
> (p. 379)

Admittedly, Hallen's argument seems interesting. But there are two possible seemingly interesting responses to the argument. One possible response comes from Wiredu himself, while the other possible response comes from Gordon Hunnings. According to Wiredu (1996), 'a human being is a rule-following animal, and language is nothing but an arrangement of rules.

Therefore, barring the impairment of faculties, any human being will necessarily have the capacity to understand and use a language … [and] any language' (p. 25). While Hunnings (1975) argues that 'un-translatability does not necessarily imply unintelligibility' (p. 13).

On the one hand, if Wiredu is right – and he is indeed right – that there is no language that non-native speakers cannot learn and use, then in spite of Hallen's argument about the imposition of English meanings by the English language speaker on other languages she learns, we can still talk about cultural universals. On the other hand, if Hunnings's argument that the inability to translate a language does not necessarily mean the language cannot be understood is apt – this argument is indeed apt – then even though the problem of translatability is about cultural particulars, the question of intelligibility points us to cultural universals.

So, in spite of Hallen's argument, and the previously mentioned arguments by the likes of Bello and Keita, I agree with Wiredu's views on the existence of cultural universals or the relationship between cultural universals and cultural particulars. I disagree with those who simultaneously agree that he is right about the existence of cultural universals but think he is wrong about the relationship between cultural universals and cultural particulars. I disagree with those who think that he misconstrues cultural universals with cultural particulars. And I disagree with those who think that the distinction between cultural universals and cultural particulars is superfluous.

In a nutshell, I disagree with those who think that the discussion on, and the reconciliation of, cultural universals and cultural particulars is a project in futility. In view of the reconciliation of cultural universals and cultural particulars, I see the possibility, and more importantly the plausibility, of reconciling cultural appropriationism with mutual exclusivism. Nevertheless, I must admit that the factors impeding such reconciliation are neither trivial nor easily tractable.

On the Conceptual Decolonisation of African Thinking

Wiredu's defence of the existence of cultural universals is not an end in itself. After arguing that cultural universals exist, he shifted his focus to what can be considered 'his most provocative set of arguments' (Wirth, 2000, p. 158). Conscious of the fact that 'it has been historically the case that cultures often coercively present particular customs and philosophical concepts as if they were universals and this was amply evident in colonialism' (p. 158), in the aforementioned provocative arguments, Wiredu deploys his Akan language – spoken in Ghana, Ivory Coast and Togo – and Akan customs to argue that 'certain philosophical problems are "tongue dependent" and that certain Western normative practices confused morality (the universal condition for the possibility of ethical behaviour) with custom (particular cultural practices that were falsely universalised)' (p. 158) (emphasis in original).

The problem, as Wirth (2000) says, is that

> colonialism fostered both the African acceptance of Western philosophical concepts often without an adequate understanding of their accompanying conceptual framework and, more distressingly, the misguided attempt to understand native African philosophical terms within a conceptual framework that is not sensitive to African 'tongue dependent' particulars.
>
> (pp. 158–159) (emphasis in original)

Consequently, for instance, when an African speaker of an African language tries to comprehend:

> their own 'tongue dependent' philosophical assumptions, but does so in English, they are falsely assuming that all philosophical terms are inter-changeable. This is not to say that English and Akan speakers cannot learn each other's terminology … but that philosophical terms come with deeply imbedded assumptions and, to understand them, one has to understand the communicative context within which they are intelligible.
>
> (Wirth, 2000, pp. 158 - 159).

In view of the aforementioned claims, and as a remedy for the aforementioned colonial malaise, Wiredu enjoins the African to rediscover her 'native communicative world' (pp. 158–159). For this reason, he is prompted to argue for the conceptual decolonisation of African thinking. Talking about conceptual decolonisation, he says:

> By this I mean the purging of African philosophical thinking of all uncritical assimilation of Western ways of thinking. That, of course, would be only part of the battle won. The other desiderata are the careful study of our own traditional philosophies and the synthesising of any insights obtained from that source with any other insights that might be gained from the intellectual resources of the modern world. In my opinion, it is only by such a reflective integration of the traditional and the modern that contemporary African philosophers can contribute to the flourishing of our peoples and, ultimately, all other peoples.
>
> (Wiredu qtd. in Oladipo, 2002, p. 328, see Osha, n.d.)

For Wiredu, conceptual decolonisation was not only theoretically plausible; it was also practicably possible. And it was not only a philosophical idea; it was also a practical project. He did not only lay

> the foundations of his project of conceptual decolonisation at the theoretical level but had also begun to explore its various practical implications by his analyses of concepts such as 'truth,' and also by his focused critique of some of the more counter-productive impacts of both colonialism and traditional culture.
>
> (Osha, n.d., sect. 2) (emphasis in original)

For this reason, through conceptual decolonisation, he campaigned for

> a re-examination of current African epistemic formations in order to accomplish two objectives. First, he wishes to subvert unsavoury aspects of indigenous traditions embedded in modern African thought so as to make it more viable. Second, he intends to undermine the unhelpful Western epistemologies to be found in African philosophical traditions.
>
> (sect. 2)

Reacting to the enduring legacy of colonialism with its residues of philosophies, concepts and cultural practices, and in view of decolonisation, Wiredu (1997) says to the African:

> try to think them through in your own African language and, on the basis of the results, review the intelligibility of the associated problems or the plausibility of the apparent solutions that have tempted you when you have pondered them in some metropolitan language.
>
> (p. I37)

Wiredu's idea of conceptual decolonisation is not novel. After all, 'in all previously colonised regions of the world, decolonisation remains a topic of considerable academic interest' (Osha, n.d., sect. 3). However, just as although the subject matter of cultural universals and cultural particulars is not novel but he approached it in a novel, innovative, interesting, and above all, insightful way, so too although the idea of conceptual decolonisation is not novel, he approached the idea in a novel, innovative, interesting, and above all, insightful way.

Moreover, it is through his theory of conceptual decolonisation that we really see what he thinks about the disagreement between cultural universals and cultural particulars. And, through his theory of conceptual decolonisation, we can make an educated guess, or safely assume what he would have said about mutual exclusivism and cultural appropriationism. Such safe assumption would not be far-fetched because his 'theory of conceptual decolonisation is essentially what defines his attitudes and gestures towards the content of contemporary African thought' (Osha, n.d., sect. 3).

My discussion on cultural universals and cultural particulars in this chapter demonstrates that cultural appropriation without the danger of falling into the metaphysical empire is possible. But this poses a problem for the decolonisation project, namely where does decolonisation begin and end or where should the project start and stop. In view of this dilemma, in the next chapter, I shall explore different pertinent issues in the decolonisation project. These issues can be summed up as a three-fold juxtaposition of cultural appropriationist and mutual exclusivist positions.

The first issue has to do with what may be possible in theory but not in practice in the decolonisation project, and this issue entails the juxtaposition of theoretical plausibility with practicable possibility. The second issue has to do with what decolonisation requires both in theory and in practice vis-à-vis the metaphysical empire, and this issue entails the juxtaposition of theoretical imperative with practical necessity, while the third issue has to do with whether to return to and retain original African languages or to appropriate and use Western languages because doing the latter is easier than the former. In this issue what I refer to as the authenticity argument is juxtaposed with what I refer to as the efficiency argument.

These issues and juxtapositions constitute the dilemma of decolonisation. But we cannot resolve the dilemma of decolonisation without answering the question of decolonisation, that is, what is the *raison d'être* of decolonisation. On the one hand, we cannot satisfactorily answer the question of decolonisation without adequately comprehending the question. On the other hand, we cannot adequately comprehend the question without first of all understanding the *raison d'être* of colonialism, that is, without understanding the logic of colonialism in the first place.

Therefore, in view of the above, I shall divide the discussion in the next chapter into three parts. In the first part, I shall discuss the *raison d'être* or logic of colonialism in order to prepare the grounds for the discussion on the *raison d'être* or question of decolonisation. In the second part, I shall discuss the *raison d'être* or question of decolonisation and explore different answers to the question. Then in the third part, I shall discuss the dilemma of decolonisation and proffer a realistic resolution to the dilemma.

Notes

1 See the description on the cover page of *Cultural Universals and Particulars: An African Perspective*. See Bibliography for full details.
2 See the description on the cover page of *Cultural Universals and Particulars: An African Perspective*. See Bibliography for full details.
3 This includes anyone who theorises about African identity and belongs to this school of thought whether she is an African or not.
4 See the description on the cover page of *Cultural Universals and Particulars: An African Perspective*. See Bibliography for full details.

Bibliography

Abraham, W. (1966) *The Mind of Africa*. Chicago, IL, The University of Chicago Press.

Anyanwu, K. C. (1983) *The African Experience in the American Market Place*. New York, Exposition Press.

Appiah, K. A. (1992) *In My Father's House: Africa in the Philosophy of Culture*. Oxford, Oxford University Press.

Bello, A. G. (2004) Some methodological controversies in African philosophy. In: Wiredu, K. (ed.) *A Companion to African Philosophy*. Malden, MA, Blackwell, pp. 259–272.

Bodunrin, P. O. (1985) Introduction. In: Bodurin, P. O. (ed.) *Philosophy in Africa: Trends and Perspectives*. Ile-Ife, University of Ife Press.

Fayemi, A. K. (2011) A critique of cultural universals and particulars in Kwasi Wiredu's philosophy. *Trames* 15, 259–276.

Grosfoguel, R. (2011) Decolonizing post-colonial studies and paradigms of political economy: Transmodernity, decolonial thinking, and global coloniality. *Transmodernity: Journal of Peripheral Cultural Production of the Luso-Hispanic World* 1 (1), 1–35.

Gyekye, K. (2011) African ethics. *The Stanford Encyclopedia of Philosophy* Fall ed. https://plato.stanford.edu/archives/fall2011/entries/african-ethics/

Hallen, B. (1995) Indeterminacy, ethno philosophy, linguistic philosophy, African philosophy. *Philosophy: Journal of the Royal Institute of Philosophy* 70 (273), 379–393.

Hountondji, P. J. (1983) *African Philosophy: Myth and Reality*, 2nd ed. Indianapolis, Indiana University Press.

Hunnings, G. (1975) Logic, language and culture. *Second Order: An African Journal of Philosophy* 4 (1), 3–13.

Keita, L. (1997) A review of Kwasi Wiredu's *Cultural Universals and Particulars*. *Quest: An International African Journal of Philosophy* 11, 171–185.

Masolo, D. A. (2005) *The Making of a Tradition: African Philosophy in the New Millennium*. Polylog, Forum for Intercultural Philosophy. http://them.polylog.org/6/amd-en.htm

Mbiti J. S. (1969) *African Religions and Philosophy*. London, Heinemann.

Mintz, S. (2018) What are values? *Ethics Sage*, August 1. https://www.ethicssage.com/2018/08/what-are-values.html

Oladipo, O. (ed.) (2002) *The Third Way in African Philosophy: Essays in Honour of Kwasi Wiredu*. Ibadan, Hope Publications.

Oruka, O. (1990) Cultural fundamentals in philosophy: Obstacles in philosophical dialogue. *Quest: An International African Journal of Philosophy* 4 (2), 31–35.

Osha, S. (n.d.) Kwasi Wiredu (1931–2022). *Internet Encyclopedia of Philosophy*. https://iep.utm.edu/wiredu/ Accessed: July 10, 2024.

Owolabi, K. (1999) Two themes in African philosophy. *Journal of Philosophy and Development* 5 (1–2), 22–33.

Senghor, L. S. (1991) Prayer to the masks. In: Dixon, M. (trans.) *The Collected Poetry*. Charlottesville, VA, University Press of Virginia.

Sodipo, O. (1975) Philosophy in Africa today. *Thought and Practice* 2 (2), 115–123.

Temples, P. (1959) *Bantu Philosophy*. Paris, Presence Africaine.

The Editors (2024) Intuition. *Encyclopedia Britannica*, July 9. https://www.britannica.com/topic/intuition

Towa, M. (1991) Conditions for the affirmation of a modern philosophical thought. In: Serequeberhan, T. (ed.) *African Philosophy: The Essential Readings*. New York, Paragon House.

Willard, J. (1970) *Cameroon Federation: Political Integration in a Fragmentary Society*. Princeton, NJ, Princeton University Press.

Wiredu, K. (1980) *Philosophy and an African Culture*. Cambridge, CambridgeUniversity Press.

Wiredu, K. (1996) *Cultural Universals and Particulars: An African Perspective*. Bloomington and Indianapolis, IN, Indiana University Press.

Wiredu, K. (1997). *Cultural Universals and Particulars: An African Perspective*. Bloomington, IN, Indiana University Press.

Wiredu, K. (2002) Conceptual decolonization as an imperative in contemporary African philosophy: Some personal reflections. *Rue Descartes* 2 (36), 53–64.

Wirth, J. M. (2000) *Cultural Universals and Particulars: An African Perspective* by Kwasi Wiredu. *The Journal of Modern African Studies* 38 (3), 511–549.

5 Resolving the Dilemma of Decolonisation

The Logic of Colonialism

As I mentioned in the concluding part of the preceding chapter, three key issues constitute the dilemma of decolonisation. My aim in this chapter is to resolve these key issues which are the juxtaposition of theoretical plausibility with practicable possibility, the juxtaposition of theoretical imperative with practical necessity and the juxtaposition of the authenticity argument with the efficiency argument.

As I explained in the preceding chapter, in the decolonisation project, the first juxtaposition is a dilemma about what may be possible in theory but not in practice; the second juxtaposition is a dilemma about what decolonisation requires both in theory and in practice vis-à-vis the metaphysical empire; and the third juxtaposition is a dilemma about whether to return to and retain original African languages or to appropriate and use Western languages because doing the latter is easier than the former.

Once again, as I mentioned in the preceding chapter, we cannot resolve the dilemma of decolonisation without answering the question of decolonisation, that is, what is the *raison d'être* of decolonisation. On the one hand, we cannot satisfactorily answer the question of decolonisation without adequately comprehending the question. On the other hand, we cannot adequately comprehend the question without first of all understanding the *raison d'être* of colonialism, that is, without understanding the logic of colonialism in the first place.

For this reason, I divide the discussion in this chapter into three parts. In the first part (this current part), I discuss the *raison d'être* or logic of colonialism in order to prepare the grounds for the discussion on the *raison d'être* or question of decolonisation. In the second part, I discuss the *raison d'être* or question of decolonisation and explore different answers to the question. Then in the third part, I discuss the dilemma of decolonisation and proffer realistic resolution to the dilemma.

DOI: 10.4324/9781003589839-5

To reiterate, it is trite to mention that without colonialism there will be no decolonisation. Even with colonialism, if colonialism were seen by all and sundry to be beneficial or benevolent, there would be no need for decolonisation. The clamour for decolonisation exists and subsists because colonialism is seen by many people in the Global South – and in the context of this book, Africa – to be an evil. To see colonialism as an evil is not to demonise colonialism or exaggerate its negative consequences. A mere cursory look, not even a thorough or careful one, at the concept, *raison d'être*, logic and *modus operandi* of colonialism suffices to see that it is indeed an evil.

Colonialism has a two-fold component, namely domination and coercion, and relying on domination and coercion, it represents a political and economic system in which some countries, especially European countries more than any other countries, USA, and Japan, but also other countries, 'explored, conquered, settled, and exploited large areas of the world' (Magdoff, Webster, & Nowell, 2023, s.p.), especially Africa, Asia, South America and Central America, but also the Caribbean and North America.

Lea Ypi (2013a) succinctly and aptly describes colonialism as 'a practice that involves both the subjugation of one people to another and the political and economic control of a dependent territory (or parts of it)' (p. 162; see Ypi, 2013b). Daniel Butt (2013) also succinctly and aptly describes it as 'a particular model of political organisation, typified by settler and exploitation colonies, and is best seen as one specific instance of imperialism, understood as the domination of a territory by a separate metropole' (p. 892).

For Butt (2013), the aforementioned domination and coercion takes three forms. In each of these three forms, the coloniser dominates and coerces the colonised in ways that are beneficial to the former but detrimental to the latter. One form of domination and coercion entails the imposition of 'rule rooted in a separate political jurisdiction' (p. 893) on the colonised by the coloniser. By so doing, the coloniser violates the colonised's right to self-determination. Another form of domination and coercion entails the imposition of the coloniser's 'culture and customs onto the colonised, whether as a result of a belief in the racial and/or cultural superiority of the colonising power … or as a mechanism for establishing and consolidating political control' (Butt, 2013, p. 893), while the final form of domination and coercion entails the exploitation of the colonised by the coloniser (Butt, 2013, p. 893).

Taking the aforementioned domination and coercion as a *fait accompli*, Ypi (2013a) thinks that it is impossible to fully comprehend colonialism without looking at three key ingredients or components that make up the phenomenon known as colonialism. Firstly, colonialism is nothing more than, and nothing less than, a practice – to conceive colonialism in any other way is a misconception, and it is to misconstrue it for something that it is not, for something else.

Secondly, being a practice, and a peculiar practice, colonialism entails the interaction of two parties who are political and collective in nature. In this interaction, one party is active while the other party is passive; that is, one party is 'doing' something while something is being done to the other party. In other words, one party is doing the domination and coercion, while the other party is being dominated and coerced. The doer is the coloniser, while the recipient of the action is the colonised.

Thirdly, the domination takes both the form of political domination and economic domination, and there are two kinds of collective political agents, namely the colonisers and the colonised (p. 162). In other words, the coloniser dominates the colonised not only politically, but also economically. In this sense, colonialism is not a mere political phenomenon or a mere economic phenomenon. It is simultaneously a political and economic phenomenon. As such, perhaps understanding it as a political-economy phenomenon is the best way to capture its essence.

So the dominating and coercive interaction between the coloniser and the colonised is aimed at the political economy advancement of the former and the political economy degradation of the latter in spite of the rhetoric of *mission civilisatrice* in the case of France, other rhetoric of civilisation and humanisation, or the rhetoric of the benevolence of European imperialism parroted by the likes of the British and American economic (and political) historian Niall Ferguson.

Note that Ypi (2013a)'s description of colonialism and its ingredients or components does not only demonstrate that colonialism is dominating and coercive. Importantly, it also demonstrates that colonialism necessarily involves an interaction and relationship between two separate political or political economy collective entities. Following this understanding of colonialism, it is not every relationship of domination and coercion that counts as colonialism. A relationship of coercion and domination is only a criterion of colonialism. For a relationship of domination and coercion to count as colonialism, the relationship must also meet other criteria; that is, it must also be a relationship between two separate collective entities. These entities are not only collective, but must also be political in nature; that is, they must also be political or political economy collective entities.

For this reason, Ypi (2013a) says that 'indigenous societies or tribal groups do count as political collectives [...whereas] individuals, family members, interest groups, or civil society associations' (p. 162) do not count. For her, 'although territoriality is descriptively crucial in distinguishing colonialism from other wrongs in the same family, it should not matter normatively' (p. 162). Put differently, as far as she is concerned, 'while political collectives are typically territorially organised, this territorial dimension is not relevant to the analysis of the wrong of colonialism' (Valentini, 2015, p. 2).

There is no doubt that the dominating and coercive relationship known as 'colonialism is associated with many all-too-familiar wrongs: oppression, exploitation, murder, racism, and dehumanisation, among others' (p. 1). Some people argue that 'the wrong of colonialism is exhausted by the "sum" of these familiar wrongs – wrongs that are not necessarily tied to colonialism, and that may also occur in non-colonial settings' (Valentini, 2015, p. 1) (emphasis in original), while other people, such as Ypi, argue that 'there is more to the wrong of colonialism.'

For Ypi, the colonial takeover and subjugation of 'political collectives are wrong as such, over and above the familiar wrongs contingently associated with such takeovers' (Valentini, 2015, p. 1). Ypi is particularly emphatic that 'colonialism always instantiates a distinctive kind of procedural wrong, one that rests on the unequal structure of the political decision procedures characterising colonial settings, rather than on their outcomes' (Valentini, 2015, p. 1).

In contradiction with the aforementioned position taken by Ypi, Laura Valentini (2015) is of the opinion that such position is implausible even though the way Ypi expresses her view is 'elegant, parsimonious and intuitively appealing' (pp. 1–2). For Valentini (2015), the position is implausible for a two-fold reason. Both reasons generally have to do with implausible interpretation, but the first reason specifically has to do with aggregate interpretation while the second reason specifically has to do with corporate interpretation (Valentini, 2015).

The problem with the aggregate interpretation is that of over-extension while the problem with the corporate interpretation is that of methodology. On the one hand, 'the aggregate interpretation over-reaches: it leads us to condemn as wrongful a range of practices that are instead justified' (Valentini, 2015, pp. 1–2). On the other hand, 'the corporate interpretation problematically presupposes that collective entities are fundamental units of moral concern, contrary to normative individualism' (Valentini, 2015, pp. 1–2).

In view of these two limitations of Ypi's position, Valentini (2015) says that

> the difficulties with Ypi's view prompt me to suggest ... that either there is no distinctive procedural wrong attached to the unilateral takeover of political collectives or, if there is, this wrong was unlikely to be instantiated in many real-world cases of colonisation ... although colonialism was wrong for countless reasons, there is no distinctive procedural wrong of colonialism.
>
> (pp. 1–2)

However, in spite of the aforementioned limitations, Ypi (2013a) is emphatic that 'the wrong of colonialism consists in the creation and upholding of a political association that denies its members equal and reciprocal terms of cooperation' (p. 158). She claims that 'for an associative offer to be considered effectively equal and reciprocal, the consent of those on the receiving end is required' (p. 179). Her claim is predicated on a prior claim by Immanuel Kant in which he claims that 'norms of equal treatment and reciprocity' (p. 173) are the regulative principles of legitimate political associations.

Given that Ypi predicated her claim on Kant's claim, if Kant is right, then Ypi is right. But if Kant is wrong, then Ypi is wrong. Assuming Kant is right and Ypi is right, that is, assuming that 'norms of equal treatment and reciprocity' (p. 173) are the regulative principles of legitimate political associations *a la* Kant, and assuming that 'for an associative offer to be considered effectively equal and reciprocal, the consent of those on the receiving end is required' (p. 179) *a la* Ypi, then colonialism is morally unjustifiable and illegitimate since the colonised never consented to be colonised by the coloniser, and more importantly, the coloniser did not interact and relate with the colonised as equal members of the same political association.

Following Kant's claim as mentioned earlier, colonialism is inherently morally unjustifiable and necessarily illegitimate since, by its nature, it is devoid of the capacity to respect 'standards of equality and reciprocity in setting up common political relations, and the consequent departure from a particular ideal of economic, social, and political association' (p. 174). For this reason, Ypi (2013a) thinks that what makes colonialism morally wrong is the fact that colonialism necessarily entails 'morally objectionable political relations' (p. 163).

From the International Covenant on Civil and Political Rights (ICCPR), to the International Covenant on Economic, Social and Cultural Rights (ICESCR), and to the Friendly Relations Declaration, the United Nations has reached a consensus on the moral unjustifiability and illegitimacy of colonialism. Through the two Covenants and Declaration, the United Nations makes its position clear on the wrong of colonialism by making categorical statements against both the practice of colonialism and the theory of colonialism.

Firstly, in both the ICCPR and ICESCR, the United Nations states that 'All peoples have the right of self-determination. By virtue of that right they freely determine their political status and freely pursue their economic, social and cultural development.' Secondly, again in both the ICCPR and ICESCR, the United Nations states that

> All peoples may, for their own ends, freely dispose of their natural wealth and resources without prejudice to any obligations arising out of international economic co-operation, based upon the principle of

> mutual benefit, and international law. In no case may a people be deprived of its own means of subsistence.

Then in the Friendly Relations Declaration, the United Nations states that

> By virtue of the principle of equal rights and self-determination of peoples enshrined in the Charter of the United Nations, all peoples have the right freely to determine, without external interference, their political status and to pursue their economic, social and cultural development, and every State has the duty to respect this right in accordance with the provisions of the Charter.
>
> (G.A. Res. 2625, XXV)

In line with the aforementioned Covenants and Declaration, Arash Abizadeh (2012) asserts that:

> The *democratic ideal* of collective self-rule is grounded in the notion that securing the conditions of individuals' autonomy and standing as equals intrinsically requires that they be the joint authors of the terms governing the political power to which they are subject. That one's interests in general are affected by others does not itself negate self-rule or autonomy and equal standing, but being unilaterally subject to a coercive and symbolic political power, without any say over the terms of its exercise, does … democratic self-rule means that the exercise of political power conforms to the collective will of those subjected to it, and … the scope-condition of democratic legitimacy is that all those subject to the exercise of political power have a right of democratic say.
>
> (p. 878) (emphasis added)

The notion of *democratic ideal*, according to Abizadeh (2012), refers to the legitimisation, or at least an attempt at the legitimisation, of 'the collective and political exercise of power, on terms respecting the equality and freedom of those over whom power is exercised, via participatory political practices of expression, contestation, discursive justification, and decision-making' (p. 880).

If the wrong of colonialism consisted only in the denial of a right to democratic say, I do not think that colonialism would have been reviled to the extent that it is reviled today. So too if the wrong of colonialism consisted only in the denial of equality and freedom, I do not think colonialism would have been reviled to the extent that it is reviled today. In non-democratic states such as China, Saudi Arabia, the United Arab Emirates, Qatar and so on, citizens or subjects do not have a right to democratic say, yet they do not revile the state the way colonialism is reviled.

In monarchical states such as Saudi Arabia, the United Arab Emirates and Qatar, citizens or subjects are denied equality, yet they do not revile the state the way colonialism is reviled. And in a state such as Saudi Arabia, the freedom of citizens or subjects is highly restricted, yet they do not revile the state the way colonialism is reviled. The fact that colonialism is reviled the way it is reviled, not only by the victims but also by the United Nations, demonstrates that the wrong of colonialism goes beyond the denial of right to democratic, say, equality and freedom.

As E. Tendayi Achiume (2019) succinctly and aptly notes, a lot has been said and 'written about the brutality and horror that Europeans visited upon the peoples they colonised' (p. 1533). From the economic underdevelopment of Africa (Rodney, 1972; French, 2021) and India (Tharoor, n.d.), to the extermination of native Americans, to the extermination of Congolese by King Leopold II, to the extermination of the Herero and Nama people of present day Namibia by the Germans, we can go on and on recounting what – more than the denial of right to democratic, say, equality and freedom – makes colonialism evil.

It is especially because of such evils as mentioned earlier that some people advocate for the rectification of the historical injustice of colonialism. As Lea Ypi, Robert E. Goodin and Christian Barry (2009) say, 'the legacy of colonialism poses huge issues of rectificatory justice' (p. 103). Even if we discount the aforementioned evils of extermination and count only the evil of economic underdevelopment, the legacy of colonialism will still warrant rectificatory justice. Again, as Ypi, Goodin and Barry (2009) say,

> imposing alien rule on people, exploiting their persons, and extracting their resources are historical wrongs crying out to be put right. That is the first thing that inevitably comes to mind when thinking about justice for former colonies, and rightly so.
>
> (p. 103)

Ypi, Goodin and Barry (2009) even go further to argue that

> alongside those issues of righting past wrongs there are further issues concerning the duties of and claims to distributive justice that people in colonial relations have with respect to one another during – and may retain after –colonial rule. On the 'associative relations' account … duties of robust distributive justice are said to be owed to all, but only, those with whom one is linked in a political association. Everyone living within the same political association has associative duties with respect to one another. That analysis is ordinarily deployed to restrict the scope of robust distributive justice narrowly to compatriots alone …. We argue, however, that those who are linked in political associations of a colonial sort have claims against one another under exactly that heading. Associative duties qua associative duties morally do not

> vary merely on account of how distant you are from those who exercise power and authority within your association. Furthermore, there are good reasons to think that at least some of those associative duties linger well beyond the colonial period itself.
>
> (p. 103) (emphasis in original)

Whether colonialism, in both its historical form and contemporary enduring legacy, warrants the application of the principles of distributive justice to the relationship between the coloniser and the colonised is not within the remit of my discussion in this book. Therefore, I will not engage Ypi, Goodin and Barry (2009)'s argument for distributive justice. Nevertheless, I think that they are apt to argue that 'the legacy of colonialism poses huge issues of rectificatory justice' (p. 103) and to conclude that the imposition of foreign rule on people, the exploitation of their persons, and the extraction of their natural and other resources are all historical injustices that are crying out for rectification. Moreover, prior to Ypi, Goodin and Barry's argument, Leif Wenar (2006) had argued, and I think that he was apt to do so, that 'if there is not a current injustice, the advocates of reparations would not make their case' (Spinner-Halev, 2012, p. 327).

The argument that the injustice of a phenomenon such as colonialism is not only historical but also current is plausible if we look at the concept and practice of colonialism carefully. Prima facie, colonialism seems to be past; that is, colonialism seemed to have ended after the political independence of the colonies. But the concept and practice of colonialism suggests that colonialism is also present. To understand the aforementioned claim, remember that colonialism is a species of the genus called imperialism. As such, as long as imperialism did not end after the political independence of the colonies, colonialism *qua* colonialism too did not end after the political independence of the colonies. As a sub-set of imperialism, colonialism has the capacity to mutate from one form of imperialism in the past to another form of imperialism in the present, and it is most likely going to mutate to yet another form of imperialism in the future.

Colonialism, as Daniel Butt (2013) insightfully explains, is 'a particular model of political organisation, typified by settler and exploitation colonies, and is best seen as *one specific instance of imperialism*, understood as the domination of a territory by a separate metropole' (p. 892) (emphasis added). Imperialism itself, as Achiume (2019) explains, is quintessentially 'the practice of empire: the projection of political and economic power beyond the territorial borders of the power-wielding political community' (p. 1541). And as the practice of empire, 'imperialism of different kinds has … structured human relations for centuries' (p. 1541).

Both Butt and Achiume are right in their conceptions of colonialism and imperialism. World history and world politics are replete with instances of colonialism and imperialism, and these instances reflect

Butt's and Achiume's conceptions of colonialism and imperialism. It is precisely because colonialism is one specific instance of imperialism *a la* Butt, and imperialism is the practice of empire *a la* Achiume, that one can categorically claim, as Ypi, Goodin and Barry (2009) do, that 'the vast majority of countries in the world have stood in an "associative relation" of a colonial sort with some other country or countries, at some time or another' (p. 103) (emphasis in original).

In the past, African states stood in colonial associative relations with European states. In the present, the former stand in neocolonial associative relations with the latter. These neocolonial associative relations entail 'the control of less-developed countries by developed countries through indirect means … a form of global power in which transnational corporations and global and multilateral institutions combine to perpetuate colonial forms of exploitation of developing countries' (Halperin, 2014, s.p.). In other words, neocolonial associative relations typify 'the stubborn persistence of colonial-era bonds tying together First and Third World peoples in an informal but very real empire, within which the latter remain subordinate to the former' (Achiume, 2019, pp. 1543–1545; see Grovogui 1996; Anghie 2012).

In his popular description of the circumstances of neocolonialism, Kwame Nkrumah (1965) says:

> Faced with the militant peoples of the ex-colonial territories in Asia, Africa, the Caribbean and Latin America, imperialism simply switches tactics. Without a qualm it dispenses with the flags, and even with certain of its more hated expatriate officials. This means, so it claims, that it is 'giving' independence to its former subjects, to be followed by 'aid' for their development. Under cover of such phrases, however, it devises innumerable ways to accomplish objectives formerly achieved by naked colonialism. It is this sum total of these modern attempts to perpetuate colonialism while at the same time talking about 'freedom,' which has come to be known as neo-colonialism.
>
> (p. 239) (emphasis in original)

Having fought for the political independence of the then Gold Coast, now Ghana, and many other African countries, Nkrumah (1965) was acutely aware that neither his country nor the rest of African countries were truly politically and economically independent. Consequently, he famously claimed that 'in the first place, the rulers of neo-colonial States derive their authority to govern, not from the will of the people, but from the support which they obtain from their neo-colonialist masters' (p. xv).

He was particularly concerned that former European colonisers (turned neo-colonisers) were still entangled with African states in colonial associative relations (turned neo-colonial associative relations). He expressed the aforementioned concern when he said that 'the essence of neo-colonialism is that the State which is subject to it is, in theory, independent and has all the outward trappings of international sovereignty. In reality its economic system and thus its political policy is directed from outside' (p. ix).

As this description of neocolonialism indicates, Nkrumah (1965) basically sees neocolonialism as a latter form of colonialism. And as the title of his book on neocolonialism suggests, he sees neocolonialism as the last stage of imperialism. He may or may not be right that neocolonialism is the last stage of imperialism. Whether he is right or wrong is one thing, and whether he was convinced that neocolonialism is the last stage of imperialism is another thing. We may doubt his prediction of the future of imperialism, but no one who is familiar with his thoughts and actions will doubt his conviction.

Both in his philosophical analysis or political theorisation on imperialism and his political practice, he worked very hard against imperialism. He saw the end of colonialism and its replacement with flag independence in his country Ghana and many other African countries, but could not see the end of neocolonialism. So, his ultimate desire to see the end of imperialism was unfulfilled or only partially fulfilled, his ultimate dream was unrealised or only partially realised, and his ultimate goal was unachieved or only partially achieved.

Just as Nkrumah worked very hard against imperialism both in his philosophical analysis or political theorisation on imperialism and his political practice, so too Karl Marx worked very hard against capitalism in his political theorisation and political economy analysis on capitalism and his political practice. Given the socialist trend in Africa during Nkrumah's time, given that Nkrumah was a notable figure and feature in the trend, given that he was influenced by Marxism and given that he was a revolutionary, he must have analysed imperialism and predicted the end of imperialism the way Karl Marx and Frederick Engels (2014; see Marx, 1992) analysed capitalism and predicted the end of capitalism.

There are two things involved in this comparison between Nkrumah and Marx and Engels, namely the analysis of a phenomenon and the prediction of the future of the phenomenon. In the case of Marx and Engels, the phenomenon analysed was capitalism and its predicted end was the replacement of capitalism with socialism due to the internal contradictions of capitalism. In the case of Nkrumah, the phenomenon analysed was imperialism and its predicted end was the replacement of neocolonialism with *real* political and economic independence. In other words, rather than the *nominal* political and economic independence which neocolonialism represents, African states (and other Global South states) will possess actual political and economic powers and freedoms. In this sense, African states (and other Global South states) will not only be able to determine their political and economic affairs in theory, they will also, and more importantly, be able to determine their political and economic affairs in practice.

Putting aside Nkrumah's prediction of the end of imperialism and whether he is right or wrong that neocolonialism is the last stage of imperialism, let us focus on his analysis of imperialism, colonialism and neocolonialism rather than his prediction. If we focus on his analysis, evidently, we will see that he does not see any substantive difference between colonialism and neocolonialism even though he recognises that the former precedes the latter. Neocolonialism is not substantially different from colonialism because neocolonialism continues the logic of colonialism by retaining 'the geopolitical terrain of colonial imperialism and colonial advantage. Neocolonial empire spans the territories of the First and Third Worlds, and is characterised by legal, political, and economic relations and institutions whose logic structurally perpetuates neocolonial advantage' (Achiume, 2019, p. 1542).

For the aforementioned reason, it is not far-fetched to argue that political independence only succeeded in shifting 'colonial empire to neocolonial empire .... The present era is defined by neocolonial imperialism, even if formal colonial imperialism has been outlawed' (p. 1541). Achiume (2019) refers to the shifting of 'colonial empire to neocolonial empire' as 'neocolonial imperialism' (p. 1541). For her, the notion of neocolonial imperialism is the most accurate way to distinguish 'the unique form of imperialism that results from the legacy, and continues the logic, of formal European colonialism from other forms of imperialism that contemporaneously exist alongside it' (p. 1541).

In the same way the logic of colonialism is retained through neocolonialism and neocolonialism continue the logic of empire, so too through the metaphysical empire, 'the immanent logic of colonialism is carried into the present by the African elite, despite its sometimes radical articulation of cultural nationalism' (Ndlovu-Gatsheni, 2018a, p. 111; see 2018b). The position of African elite is an intriguing but sad one because they pretend to have substantive political and economic powers to control the political and economic affairs of African states while it is actually their neocolonial masters that have such powers. So too they pretend to be culturally independent of Europeans while they are actually culturally dominated by Europeans.

Just as neocolonialism entails that Africans have no substantive political and economic control over their political and economic affairs, so too the carrying forward of colonial logic entails that Africans are culturally subjugated by and subservient to Europeans. As Ngugi wa Thiong'o (1986) reminds us:

> The present predicaments of Africa are often not a matter of personal choice: they arise from an historical situation. Their solutions are not so much a matter of personal decision as that of a fundamental social

> transformation of the structures of our societies starting with a real break with imperialism and its internal ruling allies. Imperialism and its comprador allies in Africa can never develop the continent.
>
> (p. xii)

The carrying forward of the logic of colonialism is not only a political and economic matter; it is also a cultural matter. For wa Thiong'o, the aforementioned cultural condition represents cultural imperialism. According to wa Thiong'o (1997),

> Cultural imperialism in the era of neo-colonialism can be a more dangerous cancer because it can take new, subtle forms. It can hide under cloaks of militant nationalism, calls for dead authenticity, performances of cultural symbolism, and even under native racist self-assertive banners that are often substitutes for national self-criticism and collective pride in the culture and history of resistance.
>
> (p. 10)

For wa Thiong'o, cultural imperialism is no less serious than political and economic imperialism. If cultural imperialism is as serious as political and economic imperialism, then we ought to be wary of the former the same way we are wary of the latter. As he says,

> The colonial process dislocates the traveler's mind from the place he or she already knows to a foreign starting point even with the body still remaining in his or her homeland. It is a process of continuous alienation from the base, a continuous process of looking at oneself from the outside of self or with the lenses of a stranger. One may end up identifying with the foreign base as the starting point towards self, that is from another self towards one-self, rather than the local being the starting point, from self to other selves.
>
> (wa Thiong'o, 2012, p. 39)

In summary, and for the purpose of reiteration, let us remember or note the following. Firstly, just as neocolonialism entails that Africans have no substantive political and economic control over their political and economic affairs, so too the carrying forward of colonial logic entails that Africans are culturally subjugated by and subservient to Europeans. Secondly, the carrying forward of the logic of colonialism is not only a political and economic matter; it is also a cultural matter. For wa Thiong'o, the aforementioned cultural condition represents cultural imperialism. Thirdly, for wa Thiong'o, cultural imperialism is no less serious than political and economic imperialism. If cultural imperialism is as serious as political and economic imperialism, then we ought to be wary of the former the same way we are wary of the latter.

In order to alert us to the danger of cultural imperialism, wa Thiong'o focuses on linguistic imperialism and narrates how European languages have 'killed' African languages both on the continent and in diaspora. In his narration, he says that 'Africans, in the diaspora and on the continent, were soon to be the recipients of this linguistic logic of conquest, with two results; linguicide in the case of the diaspora and linguistic famine, or linguifam, on the continent' (wa Thiong'o, 2009, p. 15).

He takes what he refers to as linguicide to be the equivalent of genocide. In genocide, people are exterminated, while in linguicide, the languages of the people are *exterminated*. 'Genocide involves conscious acts of physical massacre; linguicide, conscious acts of language liquidation' (p. 17). According to him, linguicide or the conscious act of language liquidation is exactly 'the fate of African languages in the diaspora' (pp. 18–20), while what he refers to as linguifam is the fate of African languages on the continent.

Although the liquidation of languages is at the heart of both linguicide and linguifam, the way of liquidation in the former is different from the way of liquidation in the latter. On the one hand, lingui-cide, as the suffix suggests, involves killing. While lingui-fam, as the suffix suggests, involves famine. In linguicide, African diaspora languages are consciously liquidated. But in linguifam, African languages on the continent are subjected to deprivation and consequently starvation (wa Thiong'o, 2009, pp. 18–20).

In his comparison of the way African diaspora languages are consciously liquidated with the way African languages are liquidated on the continent, he says:

> On the continent, languages are not liquidated in the same way. What happens to them, in the post-Berlin Conference era of direct colonialism, is linguistic famine. Linguifam is to languages what famine is to people who speak them – linguistic deprivation and, ultimately, starvation .... To starve or kill a language is to starve and kill a people's memory bank. And it is equally true that to impose a language is to impose the weight of experience it carries and its conception of self and otherness – indeed, the weight of its memory, which includes religion and education.
>
> (wa Thiong'o, 2009, pp. 18–20)

The Question of Decolonisation

Wa Thiongo's concepts of linguicide and linguifam are clearly focused on the condition of African languages both in diaspora and on the continent. Nevertheless, as already mentioned, his focus on language is a representation of his thought on cultural imperialism. Just as Nkrumah (1965) saw neocolonialism as a form of colonialism, so too wa Thiong'o sees the metaphysical empire as a form of empire. And just as Nkrumah was wary of neocolonialism, so too wa Thiong'o is wary of the metaphysical empire.

Wa Thiong'o's narration of the emergence of linguicide and linguifam in the preceding sub-chapter is akin to Nkrumah's narration of the emergence of neocolonialism. According to Nkrumah (1965),

> Faced with the militant peoples of the ex-colonial territories in Asia, Africa, the Caribbean and Latin America, imperialism simply switches tactics. Without a qualm it dispenses with the flags, and even with certain of its more hated expatriate officials. This means, so it claims, that it is 'giving' independence to its former subjects, to be followed by 'aid' for their development. Under cover of such phrases, however, it devises innumerable ways to accomplish objectives formerly achieved by naked colonialism. It is this sum total of these modern attempts to perpetuate colonialism while at the same time talking about 'freedom', which has come to be known as neo-colonialism.
>
> (p. 239) (emphasis in original)

So, if Nkrumah is right that neocolonialism is a form of colonialism, then wa Thiong'o is probably right that the metaphysical empire is a form of empire. And if Nkrumah is right that neocolonialism entails devising alternative ways to achieve the aims of colonialism, then wa Thiong'o may be right that the metaphysical empire entails linguicide and linguifam. For Nkrumah, real and actual political independence, rather than nominal and flag independence, is the solution to neocolonialism, while for wa Thiong'o, cultural independence is the solution to the metaphysical empire.

Nkrumah's position is not contentious because nearly every (this in no way means all) African both on the continent and in diaspora sees the danger of political and economic imperialism, and consequently sees the need for political and economic liberation. However, wa Thiong'o's position is contentions because while some are agreed with him that there is such thing as a metaphysical empire and it impedes cultural independence, others do not see any metaphysical empire and consequently do not see any impediment to cultural independence. For instance, Denis Ekpo (2017) thinks that:

> Decolonization of knowledge and institutions is essentially driven by a desire to get even with the oppressor and to avenge past wrongs. Rather than continue to blame imperialism for the ills of Africa, we should blame the anti-colonialist glass ceiling we have installed in our decolonialist minds. The colonization we are trying to free our minds, knowledge and institutions from is no longer in the world but purely in our minds.
>
> (s.p.)

Even more emphatic than Ekpo, Olufemi Taiwo (2022) condemns 'cultural' decolonisation. He complains that Africans have abandoned the essence of decolonisation which is political decolonisation for pseudo-decolonisation which is cultural decolonisation. He emphasises that the original intention of decolonisation was 'making a colony into a self-governing entity with its political and economic fortunes under its own direction (though not necessarily control)' (p. 2). For him, decolonisation should mean political decolonisation – no more, no less.

He thinks that the conception of decolonisation as cultural decolonisation or the stretching of the remit of decolonisation to extend from politics to culture is a misnomer. He says, departing from political decolonisation to cultural decolonisation, proponents of cultural decolonisation have misconceived decolonisation. He says the concept

> has come to mean something entirely different: forcing an ex-colony to forswear, on pain of being forever under the yoke of colonisation, any and every cultural, political, intellectual, social and linguistic artefact, idea, process, institution and practice that retains even the slightest whiff of the colonial past.
>
> (Taiwo, 2022, p. 2)

For him, the term decolonisation has become banal to the extent that it is now meaningless. For him, the use of the term decolonisation is pervasive and decolonisation permeates all spheres of thought and academic fields, and this is a testament to his claim that the term has become meaningless. As he puts it,

> the ubiquity of 'decolonisation' in all areas of thought – from literature, linguistics and philosophy, to politics, economics, sociology, psychology and medicine – indicates that either the idea packs an explanatory and/or analytical punch like no other, or it has simply become a catchall trope, often used to perform contemporary 'morality' or 'authenticity'.
>
> (Taiwo, 2022, p. 3) (emphasis in original)

Without hesitation, he categorically states that he is 'convinced that the latter is increasingly the case' (Taiwo, 2022, p. 3).

An example of the over-extension of the concept of decolonisation (the kind of decolonisation that Ekpo and Taiwo would criticise) is Peter Ekeh (1975)'s reductionistic view of decolonisation as a matter of the relationship between African elites and European colonisers. According to Ekeh (1975),

> In many ways, the drama of colonization is the history of the clash between the European colonisers and African bourgeois class. Although native to Africa, the African bourgeois class depends on

> colonialism for its legitimacy. It accepts the principles implicit in colonialism but it rejects the foreign personnel that rule Africa. It claims to be competent enough to rule, but it has no traditional legitimacy. In order to replace the colonisers and rule its own people, it invented a number of interest-begotten theories to justify that rule.
>
> (p. 96)

Another example of the over-extension of the concept of decolonisation (the kind of decolonisation that Ekpo and Taiwo would criticise) is Achiume (2019)'s departure from an institutionalist conception of decolonisation to an individualist conception of decolonisation. In her individualist conception of decolonisation, Achiume (2019) acknowledges that 'in international law and legal theory, decolonisation is a process for political collectives: Individuals are neither the subjects nor the objects of decolonisation; nation-states are' (p. 1522). However, she explains that her argument

> is that the political equality claims that nation-state decolonization is designed to vindicate may have to be pursued through alternative means, including through individual rather than purely structural approaches. Given the failure of formal independence to undo colonial subordination, for some Third World persons, so-called economic migration may enact a process that enhances individual self-determination within neocolonial empire, irrespective of its implications for the collective self-determination of Third World nation-states. This personal pursuit of enhanced self-determination (which asserts political equality with First World citizens) is thus decolonial; it is migration as decolonization.
>
> (Achiume, 2019, p. 1522)

Furthermore, she explains that the objective of her individualist conception of decolonisation

> is not to offer a tidy, ideal theory of how decolonisation can be achieved for all peoples everywhere. Rather, it is to reframe migration – even unauthorised Third World migration – as one compelling means of asserting individual agency over political horizons, and to argue for the formal recognition in the law of this expression of agency.
>
> (Achiume, 2019, p. 1522)

No matter how novel, innovative and elegant Achiume's individualist conception of decolonisation appears, the fact that she departs from the original conception of decolonisation which is institutionalist means that her conception cannot deal with collectives. And the fact that her conception cannot deal with collectives means that it is not suitable for the resolution of the colonial and neocolonial institutional problems that collectives on the continent and in diaspora face.

It is almost self-evident that the individualist conception of decolonisation is reductionistic. In other words, even though Achiume 'is not concerned with methodological individualism, the sole focus on the individualist approach is reductionistic because it is tantamount to methodological individualism' (Abumere, 2020, p. 279). Methodological individualism, as Joseph Heath (2005) explains, posits that 'social phenomena must be explained by showing how they result from individual actions, which in turn must be explained through reference to the intentional states that motivated the individual actors' (intro.).

If Taiwo were to criticise Ekeh's African elites/European colonisers relations view of decolonisation and Achiume's individualist conception of decolonisation for over-extending the concept of decolonisation, I think Taiwo would be right and I would totally agree with him. However, I think Taiwo went too far to claim that cultural decolonisation is unnecessary. Although I disagree with him that cultural decolonisation is unnecessary, I agree with him that the meaning of the term decolonisation has been over-extended by proponents of decolonisation. To his credit, I think he is likely to be apt when he claims that a lot of the objectives that proponents of cultural decolonisation want to use the concept of decolonisation to achieve do not need the deployment of the concept before those objectives can be achieved. As he says, a lot of the tasks the concept is deployed to do are either already being done or can be done without the invocation of the buzzword of decolonisation 'and without some of the histrionics that go with it' (Taiwo, 2022).

Like Ekpo and Taiwo, Ato Sekyi-Otu (1996) also thinks that the departure from political decolonisation to cultural decolonisation is a misnomer. More than Taiwo, and far more than Ekpo, Sekyi-Otu castigates the proponents of cultural decolonisation. For him, the misnomer of misconstruing decolonisation for cultural decolonisation or of extending the remit of decolonisation to cover cultural decolonisation is not only an African problem but a Global South problem. So, he does not restrict his castigation to African proponents of decolonisation; he extends it to Global South proponents of decolonisation. He says that

> such is the vicious paradox of some critiques of 'universalism' from Africa and the global South: their obsessive-compulsive Eurocentrism; their willful captivity to the very discourse they are avowedly sworn to divulge and dethrone; their exclusive preoccupation with the things the West does with words in order to enforce its particulars as universals; their trained habit, in contrast, of being utterly incurious regarding what our grandmothers do with words of evaluative judgment that have universals for their predicates. It is as if purveyors of Eurocentrism

> and their critics drink from the same cup and end up inebriated in separate beds but with kindred distractions. That must be the reason why 'universalism' is chief among those ritual anathemas of anti-imperialism or, as they say 'counterhegemonic' discourse.
>
> (Sekyi-Otu, 1996, pp. 14–15) (emphasis in original)

From Ekpo, to Taiwo to Sekyi-Otu, we get the impression that cultural decolonisation is a bad thing. If we only listen to their views without listening to counter-views such as Frantz Fanon's, we might remain with such impression. Even if listening to counter-views such as Fanon's does not totally change the mind of someone who already sees cultural decolonisation as a bad thing and make her see it as a good thing, it might make her see it differently and at least second-guess her impression. Seeing cultural decolonisation differently might mean seeing it to be neutral or at least to be less bad than Ekpo, Taiwo and Sekyi-Otu want us to believe it is.

Fanon (1961) thinks that it is only when we situate decolonisation within a historical context and realise that decolonisation is a historical process rather than an ahistorical phenomenon that we will truly grasp what decolonisation is all about. For him, realising that decolonisation is a historical process entails detecting or recognising the historical *zeitgeisten*[1] that shapes the scope and content of decolonisation. For Fanon (1961), decolonisation, in the above sense,

> cannot be understood, it cannot become intelligible nor clear to itself except in the exact measure that we can discern the movements which give it historical form and content ... decolonisation never takes place unnoticed, for it influences individuals and modifies them fundamentally. It transforms spectators crushed with their inessentiality into privileged actors, with the grandiose glare of history's floodlights upon them. It brings a natural rhythm into existence, introduced by *new men*, and with it a *new language* and a *new humanity*. Decolonisation is the veritable creation of *new men*.
>
> (pp. 28–29) (emphasis in original)

Situating decolonisation in the context of history, Sabelo J. Ndlovu-Gatsheni (2019) explains the imperative. Specifically, from a mutual exclusivist perspective, he explains the imperative of decolonisation, why appropriationism should be rejected and why wholesale cultural decolonisation is the way forward. He argues that there are 'six broad imperatives that invite us to define and explain decolonisation/decoloniality in the twenty-first century' (s.p.).

Firstly, he argues that there is the re-emergence of the 'idea that the empire especially the British Empire was benevolent resulting in attempts by some scholars to draw a "balance sheet" of the impact of colonialism particularly its benefits' (Ndlovu-Gatsheni, 2019, s.p.) (emphasis in original). Secondly, he argues that a strong belief exists

> in some circles that decolonisation struggles were a twentieth century phenomenon and they delivered liberation of the colonised people, so the harking back to the sins and evils of colonialism is nothing but an attempt to compensate for African failures to govern themselves.
>
> (Ndlovu-Gatsheni, 2019, s.p.)

Thirdly, he argues that a strong tendency is noticeable particularly 'among those who are beneficiaries of the current status quo to caricature rather than seek to make sense of the struggles for decolonisation as nothing but being stuck in the past' (Ndlovu-Gatsheni, 2019, s.p.). Fourthly, he argues that there is, undeniably, evident 'resurgence and insurgence of decolonisation/decoloniality provoking an urgent need for clarification of concepts and theories as well as exploration of its practical applications particularly in institutions of higher education and in wider society' (Ndlovu-Gatsheni, 2019, s.p.).

Fifthly, he argues that, seemingly,

> the current decolonisation struggles are mainly pivoted on epistemological questions, thus making universities legitimate sites of struggles and this has generated a need to explain what decolonisation means for the institutions of higher education, knowledge, curriculum, pedagogy, institutional cultures, and funding of universities.
>
> (Ndlovu-Gatsheni, 2019, s.p.)

Finally, he poses a question 'whether decolonisation/decoloniality is the most appropriate vehicle to carry us into a better future free from racism, domination and inequalities' (Ndlovu-Gatsheni, 2019, s.p.).

In view of the question of decolonisation, Ndlovu-Gatsheni (2018a, 2018b) proposes the decentring of Europe and centring Africa. His proposal entails 'complex dimensions of epistemological decolonisation, and the equally complex circulation of knowledge' (p. 107). Like his imperatives of decolonisation as discussed earlier, his dimensions of decolonisation are six in number. The six dimensions of decolonisation in turn have six explanatory notes.

In his first dimension of decolonisation, he proposes the provincialisation of Europe and the de-provincialisation of Africa, that is, moving Europe to the periphery while moving Africa to the centre. He explains that such provincialisation and de-provincialisation

> entails two moves: restoration of Africa as a legitimate epistemic site of knowledge, and taking seriously African knowledge as a departure

> point without necessarily throwing away knowledge from Europe and North America. The purpose is to deal with the crisis of relevance and alienation. It is a restorative move that enable Africans to see themselves clearly. It entails shifting of a position from which Africans know and interpret the world.
>
> (Ndlovu-Gatsheni, 2018a, p. 107; see wa Thiong'o, 1986)

He says that on the one hand, while other decolonial theorists such as the Asian decolonial theorist Dipesh Chakrabarty (2000) stress the idea of the provincialisation of Europe, 'African decolonial theorists of the twenty-first century are pushing for "deprovincialising Africa," making it a centre after centuries of peripherisation' (Ndlovu-Gatsheni, 2018a, p. 108; see Mbembe, 2017) (emphasis in original).

In his second dimension of decolonisation, he proposes the Africanisation of knowledge. He explains that

> this entails re-assertion of African identity and re-founding of knowledge on African cultures and values. It is a recovery process predicated on ideas of endogenous knowledge as an internal product drawn from a given cultural background, as opposed to another category of knowledge which would be imported from elsewhere.
>
> (Ndlovu-Gatsheni, 2018a, p. 108; see Hountondji, 1997, p. 17)

In his third dimension of decolonisation, he proposes 'adding/including African knowledge into the existing canon of knowledge' (Ndlovu-Gatsheni, 2018a, p. 108). Then he explains that 'this is a poor form of decolonisation which takes the lazy format of just adding new items to the existing canon and existing curriculum. The pre-occupation here is with adding new content without re-configuring the curriculum' (Ndlovu-Gatsheni, 2018a, p. 108).

In the fourth dimension of decolonisation, he proposes 'decolonial critical engagement with existing knowledge' (Ndlovu-Gatsheni, 2018a, p. 108). Then in his explanatory note, he says that

> this approach entails deep questioning of 'received' knowledge and critical engagement with the politics of knowledge production and dissemination. This approach seeks to unmask the concealed problems such as racism and embedded asymmetrical power dynamics. Decolonial critical engagement with existing knowledge must also involve questioning even endogenous knowledge in the manner Hountondji did when he raised the problem of unanimity and collectivity in what became known as 'ethnophilosophy'.
>
> (Ndlovu-Gatsheni, 2018a, p. 108)

In the fifth dimension of decolonisation, he proposes 'nativism and ghettoisation of knowledge' (p. 108). Then in his explanatory note, he says:

> This is a very poor understanding of epistemological decolonisation as that of delinking and self-enclosure informed by racial essentialisation of identity to the extent of reproducing that which colonialism imposed such as chauvinism, racism, sexism, and xenophobia .... The unfortunate result is what one can term 'epistemic xenophobia,' which impoverishes knowledge rather than enriching it.
>
> (Ndlovu-Gatsheni, 2018a, p. 109; see Fanon, 1968; Jansen, 2017, pp. 167–169)

Finally, in the sixth dimension of decolonisation, he proposes the democratisation of knowledge or ecologies of knowledge (Ndlovu-gatsheni, 2018a, p. 109). Then in his explanatory note, he says that 'this entails opening up of the academy to a plurality of knowledges including the subjugated ones as part of the achievement of cognitive justice' (Ndlovu-Gatsheni, 2018a, p. 109; see Santos, 2014). The aforementioned democratisation of knowledge, he says, is aimed at creating a friendly intellection and theorisation which is expected to engage in a confrontation with, and overcome, 'the challenge of over-prescription, over-standardisation, over-routinisation and over-prediction' (Nyamnjoh, 2017, p. 5; see Ndlovu-Gatsheni, 2018a, p. 109).

The Dilemma of Decolonisation

Having dealt with the question of decolonisation in the preceding sub-chapter, I will shift focus to resolving the issues I set out to resolve at the beginning of this chapter. Remember that the first issue has to do with what may be possible in theory but not in practice in the decolonisation project, and this issue entails the juxtaposition of theoretical plausibility with practicable possibility. The second issue has to do with what decolonisation requires both in theory and in practice vis-à-vis the metaphysical empire, and this issue entails the juxtaposition of theoretical imperative with practical necessity. While the third issue has to do with whether to return to and retain original African languages or to appropriate and use Western languages because doing the latter is easier than the former. In this issue what I refer to as the authenticity argument is juxtaposed with what I refer to as the efficiency argument.

The discussion on the question of decolonisation already suggests the way I will respond to the aforementioned issues. Regarding the first issue which has to do with what may be possible in theory but not in practice in the decolonisation project, that is, the juxtaposition of theoretical plausibility with practicable possibility, I think that decolonisation is simultaneously theoretically plausible and practicably possible. However, my affirmative response comes with a caveat; that is, my response does not stand *sui generis*; it comes with a qualification. Using decolonisation *tout court* is the quickest and easiest way to fall into the danger of over-extending the concept.

I do not think that decolonisation is the *sine qua non* and the *conditio per quam* for the political, economic and cultural progress of the continent. However, I think that decolonisation is vital in our self-conception as Africans, and in re-imagining our place in world history and world politics. For instance, as some people have pointed out, naming, describing and identifying different African people based on the language of their colonisers is an affront on the self-conception of people who have their own original languages. Why call some Africans Anglophone, some Francophone, others Lusophone and so on, simply because they inherited and speak the English, French and Portuguese or Spanish and Arabic languages from their colonisers even when the majority of Africans speak their own original languages? The answer to these questions lies in what the famous Nigerian musician, originator of Afrobeat and human rights activist, Fela Anikulapo Kuti calls colonial mentality.

To have a colonial mentality, *a la* Fela, is to see oneself through the prism of colonialism. This means that a people that were once colonised refuse or fail to jettison their colonial conditioning. Even when they live in Lagos, Abidjan, Maputo and Kinshasa, they imagine themselves living in, and consequently behave as if they were living in, London, Paris, Lisbon and Brussels. In a situation like this, cultural decolonisation is theoretically plausible because it helps to reset the African mindset in order for the African to regain the lost capacity of valuing her own original culture and not seeing it as inferior to European cultures.

In a situation like this, decolonisation is not only theoretically plausible, but also practically possible. For instance, in Nigerian television stations, radio stations and airports, the presenters, newscasters, On Air Personalities (OAPs), DJs and announcers who speak with funny and forced (funny and forced because they are not even true representative) America, British and other *mélange* foreign accents should be advised to stop their poor act of mimicry and encourage to speak 'properly' and speak in a way that people, their viewers and listeners will understand without straining their ears.

Regarding the second issue which has to do with what decolonisation requires both in theory and in practice vis-à-vis the metaphysical empire, that is, the juxtaposition of theoretical imperative with practical necessity, I think that the question of decolonisation should not lend itself to the Kantian saying that this may be possible in theory but not in practice.[2] My 'qualified' decolonisation or decolonisation with a caveat recognises and respects the limit of decolonisation when its theory is applied in practice.

One problem with mutual exclusivists is that the kind of decolonisation they advocate for is susceptible to being true in theory but not applicable in practice. To advocate for wholesale decolonisation of culture is to forget that cultural is dynamic rather than static. As I have already mentioned, a static culture is a dead culture and a dynamic culture is a living culture. A people that values its culture can still borrow and integrate some aspects of foreign culture into its culture – after all, we all know that culture is dynamic rather than static; a static culture is a dead culture and a dynamic culture is a living culture. And an African people that values its language can still use European languages. But it should not jettison its original language because it thinks European languages are superior to original African languages.

Regarding the third issue which has to do with whether to return to and retain original African languages or to appropriate and use Western languages because doing the latter is easier than the former – that is, the juxtaposition of the authenticity argument with the efficiency argument – a combination of my responses to the first and second issues suffice as my response. I accept that, for instance, since the English language is the most spoken language in the world, using the language has its advantages especially in a world that is globalised with the kind of extensity, intensity and velocity that we have never seen before. However, small countries (population-wise) such as Norway and the Netherlands retain Norwegian and Dutch, respectively, even when a size-able number of their citizens are capable of speaking the English language.

What the examples of Norway and the Netherlands demonstrate is that a people that values its culture can still borrow and integrate some aspects of foreign culture into its culture – after all, to reiterate, we all know that culture is dynamic rather than static; a static culture is a dead culture and a dynamic culture is a living culture. And an African people that values its language can still use European languages. But it should not jettison its original language because it thinks European languages are superior to original African languages.

My responses to these three issues may not be self-evidently middle-of-the-road between the extreme of mutual exclusivism and the extreme of cultural appropriationism because they seem to tilt towards the latter. However, my position as contained in the responses is clearly different from the positions of champions of mutual exclusivism such as Ngugi wa Thiong'o and champions of cultural appropriationism such as Chinua Achebe. On the one hand, Chinua Achebe 'argued that English allowed for communicating across the different African languages while also reaching wider audiences in the West; that it was the language of power; that English could be Africanised so that it carried the African experience' (wa Ngugi, 2018, s.p.). On the other hand, Ngugi wa Thiong'o (2016) argues that

> a return to the base, for the people, must mean at the very least the use of a language and languages that the people speak. Any further linguistic additions should be for strengthening, deepening and widening this power of the languages spoken by the people.
>
> (pp. 49–50)

People like wa Thiong'o are particularly wary of the appropriation of European languages because they see such appropriation as a gateway to the colonisation, neocolonisation, re-colonisation or continuous colonisation of African cultures by European cultures. As such, for them, European languages represent European cultural hegemony and appropriation of European languages is cultural imperialism *tout court*. They are convinced that

> what constitutes the West more than geography is a linguistic family, a belief system and an epistemology. It is constituted by six modern European and imperial languages: Italian, Spanish and Portuguese, which were dominant during the Renaissance, and English, French and German, which have been dominant since the Enlightenment.
>
> (Mignolo, 2015, pp. xxv–xxvi)

Notes

1 *Zeitgeisten* is the German plural of the singular *zeitgeist*.
2 See Immanuel Kant (1793)'s *On the Common Saying: That May be Correct in Theory but it is of no use in Practice*. See Bibliography for full details.

Bibliography

Abizadeh, A. (2012) On the demos and its kin: Nationalism, democracy, and the boundary problem. *American Political Science Review* 106 (4), 867–882.

Abumere, F. A. (2020) The problem with the individualist approach to the principle of the immunity of non-combatants. *South African Journal of Philosophy* 39 (3), 274–284.

Achiume, E. T. (2019) Migration as decolonisation. *Stanford Law Review* 71, 1509–1574.

Anghie, A. (2012). *Imperialism, Sovereignty and the Making of International Law*. Cambridge, Cambridge University Press.

Butt, D. (2013) Colonialism and postcolonialism. In: LaFollette, H. (ed.) *The International Encyclopedia of Ethics*, 2nd ed., s.p. Hoboken, New Jersey, John Wiley and Sons.

Chakrabarty, D. (2000). *Provincializing Europe: Postcolonial Thought and Historical Difference*. Princeton, NJ, Princeton University Press.

Ekeh, P. P. (1975) Colonialism and the two publics in Africa: A theoretical statement. *Comparative Studies in Society and History* 17 (1), 96–123.

Ekpo, D. (2017) *Freeing the African mind more complex than simply decolonisation – fellows' seminar by Denis Ekpo, STIAS – Stellenbosch Institute for Advanced Study*, Stellenbosch University, Stellenbosch, South Africa, October 9. https://stias.ac.za/2017/10/freeing-the-african-mind-more-complex-than-simply-decolonisation/

Fanon, F. (1961) *The Wretched of the Earth*. London, Penguin.

Fanon, F. (1968). *The Wretched of the Earth*. New York, Grove Atlantic.

French, H. W. (2021) *Born in Blackness: Africa, Africans, and the Making of the Modern World, 1471 to the Second World War*. New York, Liveright.

Grovogui, S. N. (1996) *Sovereigns, Quasi Sovereigns and Africans: Race and Self-Determination in International Law*. Minneapolis, MN, University of Minnesota Press.

Halperin, S. (2014) Neocolonialism. *Encyclopedia Britannica*. www.britannica.com/topic/neocolonialism

Heath, J. (2005). Methodological individualism. In: *Stanford Encyclopedia of Philosophy*, Winter ed. http://plato.stanford.edu/entries/methodological-individualism/

Hountondji, P. J. (1997) Introduction: Recentring Africa. In: Hountondji, P. J. (ed.) *Endogenous Knowledge: Research Trails*. Dakar, CODESRIA, pp. 1–39.

Jansen, J. (2017) *As by Fire: The End of the South African University*. Cape Town, Tafelberg.

Kant, I. (1793[2012]). *On the Common Saying: That May be Correct in Theory but It Is of No Use in Practice*. Edited by Mary J. Gregor. Cambridge, Cambridge University Press.

Magdoff, H., Webster, R. A. & Nowell, C. E. (2023) Western colonialism. *Encyclopedia Britannica*, December 18. https://www.britannica.com/topic/Western-colonialism

Marx, K. (1992). *Early Writings*. Translated by Rodney Livingstone and Gregor Benton. London, Penguin Books.

Marx, K. & Engels, F. (2014) *The Communist Manifesto*. New York, International Publishers.

Mbembe, A. (2017) *Critique of Black Reason*. Dubois, L. (trans). Durham, NC, Duke University Press.

Mignolo, W. D. (2015) Foreword: Yes, we can. In: Dabashi, H. (eds.) *Can Non-Europeans Think?* London, Zed Books, pp. viii–xlii.

Ndlovu-Gatsheni, S. J. (2018). Metaphysical empire, linguicide and cultural imperialism. *English Academy Review* 35 (2), 96–115.

Ndlovu-Gatsheni, S. J. (2018a) Metaphysical empire, linguicides and cultural imperialism. *English Academy Review* 35 (2), 96–115.

Ndlovu-Gatsheni, S. J. (2018b) *Epistemic Freedom in Africa: Deprovincialisation and Decolonisation*. London, Routledge.

Ndlovu-Gatsheni, S. J. (2019) The struggles for epistemic freedom and the decolonisation of knowledge in Africa. *Webinar Lecture delivered at the Convivial Thinking Collective in collaboration with European Association of Development Research and Training Institutes (EADI)*, March 12. https://www.eadi.org/fileadmin/user_upload/EADI/05_Development_Studies/Virtual_Dialogue/EADI_Webinar_12_-_The_Struggles_of_Epistemic_Freedom_and_Decolonization_of_Knowledge_in_Africa__2019-03-12_.pdf

Nkrumah, K. (1965) *Neo-colonialism*. London, Thomas Nelson.

Nyamnjoh, F. B. (2017) *Drinking from the Cosmic Gourd: How Amos Tutuola Can Change Our Minds*. Bamenda, Langaa Research & Publishing CIG.

Rodney, W. (1972) *How Europe Underdeveloped Africa*. Nairobi, East African Educational Publishers.

Santos, B. (2014) *Epistemologies of the South: Justice against Epistemicide*. Boulder, CO, Paradigm Publishers.

Sekyi-Otu, A. (1996) *Fanon's Dialectic of Experience*. Cambridge, MA, Harvard University Press.

Spinner-Halev, J. (2012) Historical injustice. In: Estlund, D. (ed.) *The Oxford Handbook of Political Philosophy*. Oxford, Oxford University Press, pp. 319–335.

Taiwo, O. (2022) *Against Decolonisation: Taking African Agency Seriously*. London, Hurst & Company.

United Nations (General Assembly) (1966a) *International Covenant on Civil and Political Rights*. Treaty Series, 999, 171. New York, USA, UN Headquarters.

United Nations (General Assembly) (1966b) International covenant on economic, social, and cultural rights. *Treaty Series* 999 (December), 171. UN Headquarters, New York, USA.

United Nations (UN) (1970) General Assembly resolution 2625 – G.A. Res. 2625 – (XXV), Declaration on principles of international law concerning friendly relations and co-operation among states in accordance with the charter of the United Nations declaration, at 123 (Oct. 24, 1970), UN Headquarters, New York, USA.

Valentini, L. (2015) On the distinctive procedural wrong of colonialism. *Philosophy and Public Affairs* 43 (4), pp. 312–331.

Wa Ngugi, M. (2018) What decolonising the mind means today. Literary Hub, March 23. https://lithub.com/mukoma-wa-ngugi-what-decolonizing-the-mind-means-today/

Wa Thiong'o, N. (1986) *Decolonising the Mind: The Politics of Language in African Literature*. Oxford, James Currey.

Wa Thiong'o, N. (1997) *Writers in Politics: A Re-Engagement with Issues of Literature and Society*. Oxford, James Currey.

Wa Thiong'o, N. (2009) *Some Thing Torn and New: An African Renaissance*. New York, Basic Civitas Books.

Wa Thiong'o, N. (2012) *Globalectics: Theory and the Politics of Knowing*. New York, Columbia University Press.

Wa Thiong'o, N. (2016) *Secure the Base: Making Africa Visible in the Globe*. London, Seagull Books.

Wenar, L. (2006) Reparations for the future. *Journal of Social Philosophy* 37 (3), 396–405.

Ypi, L. (2013a) What's wrong with colonialism. *Philosophy and Public Affairs* 41 (2): 158–191.

Ypi, L. (2013b) Territorial rights and exclusion. *Philosophy Compass* 8 (3): 241–253.

Ypi, L., Goodin, R. E. & Barry, C. (2009) Associative duties, global justice, and the colonies. *Philosophy and Public Affairs* 37 (2), 103–135.

6 Conclusion

The Decolonisation Fallacy and Fusion of Horizons

The Decolonisation Fallacy

In the preceding chapter, I explained that the three issues and juxtapositions that I resolved in the chapter constitute the dilemma of decolonisation. In the chapter, I noted that we cannot resolve the dilemma of decolonisation without answering the question of decolonisation, that is, what is the *raison d'être* of decolonisation. On the one hand, we cannot satisfactorily answer the question of decolonisation without adequately comprehending the question. On the other hand, we cannot adequately comprehend the question without first of all understanding the *raison d'être* of colonialism, that is, without understanding the logic of colonialism in the first place.

Therefore, in the preceding chapter, I began my quest of answering the question of decolonisation and resolving the dilemma of decolonisation by discussing the *raison d'être* or logic of colonialism in order to prepare the grounds for the discussion on the *raison d'être* or question of decolonisation. I continued by discussing the *raison d'être* or question of decolonisation and explored different answers to the question. Then I concluded by discussing the dilemma of decolonisation and proffering a realistic resolution to the dilemma.

Since the three issues, and the consequent juxtapositions, I resolved in the preceding chapter sum up the dilemma of decolonisation, resolving them means resolving the dilemma of decolonisation. To reiterate, I think that in view of the issues and juxtapositions, what the dilemma of decolonisation suggests is that even in the face of the danger of the metaphysical empire, the decolonisation project can still be accommodative. An accommodative decolonisation, recognising the relationship between cultural universals and cultural particulars, simultaneously promotes the originality and authenticity of African cultures and creates room for cultural appropriation because it sees certain things as human achievement rather than African, European, American, Asian, Arabic or Chinese achievement.

DOI: 10.4324/9781003589839-6

While mutual exclusivists are interested in absolute or extreme decolonisation, accommodative decolonisation is interested in 'qualified' decolonisation, that is, decolonisation with a caveat as I explained in the preceding chapter. While mutual exclusivists' kind of decolonisation proverbially throws the baby out with the bathwater, my qualified decolonisation or decolonisation with a caveat recognises the dynamism of culture and thus borrows and integrates some elements of Western cultures into African cultures if and only if those elements are helpful.

For instance, as I argued in the preceding chapter, an African can speak the English language when communicating with foreigners (just as a Norwegian or a Dutch does) due to the demands of globalisation but she should retain her original language and never jettison it for English. Kwasi Wiredu (1995) takes the same position when he says 'until Africa can have a lingua franca, we will have to communicate suitable parts of our work in our multifarious vernaculars, and in other forms of popular discourse, while using the metropolitan languages for international communication' (p. 20).

Since my accommodative decolonisation seems to tilt towards cultural appropriationism, it is easier to convince cultural appropriationists to accept it than to convince mutual exclusivists to accept it. However, it is not impossible to convince mutual exclusivists to accept it because even the chief architect of mutual exclusivism Ngugi wa Thiong'o (1993) envisages a situation in which:

> African languages will borrow from one another; they will borrow from their classical heritages; they will borrow from the world – from the Caribbean, from Afro-American, from Latin American, from the Asian – and from the European worlds. In this, the new writing in African languages will do the opposite of the Europhone practice: instead of being appropriated by the world, it will appropriate the world and one hopes on terms of equal exchange, at the very least borrow on its own terms and needs.
>
> (p. 23)

Furthermore, I think it is not impossible to convince mutual exclusivists to accept it because as a popular mutual exclusivist, Sabelo J. Ndlovu-Gatsheni (2018), says, 'the decoloniality intellectual framework is not against "the universal" per se' (p. 102) (emphasis in original). After all, 'decoloniality theorists have coined the term "pluriversality" in their attempt to name a new world in which diverse forms of life and living will be accommodated' (Ndlovu-Gatsheni, 2018, p. 103; see Mignolo, 2011).

Since mutual exclusivists are not against the universal, and since they accept pluriversality, accommodative decolonisation is not really their problem; what they are really concerned about is injustice. Coming from the Global South, especially Africa, mutual exclusivists should not be blamed for seeing anything European or Western as a special purpose vehicle for injustice designed by Europeans or Westerners to perpetuate their mission and acts of injustice against Africans and Global Southerners. Moreover, it is evident that our world is characterised by global inequality and injustice. It is not contentious to say that such inequality and injustice are evident in the relationship between the Global North and the Global South. And it is a *fait accompli* that, being the poorest region in the Global South, Africa is especially at the receiving end of such inequality and injustice.

Global social, political and economic inequality and injustice pervade the contemporary world. It may not be contentious to assert that such inequality and injustice characterise Global North-Global South relations both at the institutional level (rules, norms and practices that shape and regulate the relationship between the former or its members, states and organisations and the latter or its members, states and organisations) and interactional level (between the citizens of the former and the citizens of the latter). It may even be less contentious to assert that it is a *fait accompli* that such interactional and institutional inequality and injustice especially affects African states and citizens. In other words, since Africa is the poorest region in the world, since African states are the poorest states in the world and since Africans are the poorest people in the world, they are the region, states and people that are usually and always, or at least mostly, at the receiving end of such interactional and institutional inequality and injustice.

Moreover:

> In our world today, and on the African continent, there are abundant … international and global cases of injustice that are not remedied. The lack of remedy is largely, or at least partly, because there is a consensus – implicit or explicit – among relevant national, international and global political actors not to destabilise the *status quo* in world politics. Since remedying the injustices may lead to the destabilisation of the *status quo*, the relevant global political actors choose the 'lesser evil' of ignoring the injustices rather than the 'greater evil' of destabilising the *status quo*. Consequently, while there are abundant cases of injustice in global politics, there are no abundant cases of justice. In world politics, there are no shortages of injustice; there are only shortages of justice.
>
> (Abumere, 2022, p. 98) (emphasis in original)

Basically, the pattern of the division of the advantages and disadvantages that are generated by global economic and political interaction and cooperation or competition is skewed in favour of the globally well-off and to the detriment of the globally worse-off. The well-off is the Global North, while the worse-off is the Global South. Since Africa is the poorest region in the Global South, African and Africans are the most globally economically and economically disadvantaged region and people in the world. For this reason, cultural appropriationists, like mutual exclusivists, should be worried about global inequality and injustice, and such global inequality and injustice should prompt both cultural appropriationists and mutual exclusivists to revisit the dominant theoretical approaches to global inequality and injustice.

I contend that neither the mutual exclusivist nor the cultural appropriationist approach to the problem of the metaphysical empire in particular and the problem of global inequality and injustice in general is simultaneously necessary and sufficient to address such problems. In my contribution to the debate between mutual exclusivists and cultural appropriationists, my objective is not to endorse the view of one side and oppose the view of the other, but rather to integrate both views in order to develop a more robust approach. By leveraging the strengths of mutual exclusivism to compensate for the weaknesses of cultural appropriationism and vice versa, my aim is to propose a new middle-of-the road approach that can effectively tackle the problem of the metaphysical empire.

Instead of delving into the application of my middle-of-the-road approach to a specific instance of the metaphysical empire, my argument in this book demonstrates the characteristics of a new middle of the road approach designed to tackle the general problem of the metaphysical empire. In a colloquial sense, one may perceive mutual exclusivism as a thesis, cultural appropriationism as an antithesis, and the amalgamation of both mutual exclusivism and cultural appropriationism as a synthesis, akin to Hegelian dialectics. This synthesis is what I refer to as accommodative decolonisation – or middle-of-the-road approach, qualified decolonisation and decolonisation with a caveat.

In view of my accommodative decolonisation, I think that both cultural appropriationists and mutual exclusivists must simultaneously renounce absolutism (this does not mean they should embrace relativism) and be amenable to fusion of horizons. By arguing that both cultural appropriationists and mutual exclusivists must simultaneously renounce absolutism (this does not mean they should embrace relativism) and be amenable to fusion of horizons, and by proposing fusion of horizons as the way forward for the discourse on the metaphysical empire, I avoid what I refer to as the decolonisation fallacy which is tantamount to arguing that things are always either/or.

The debate on the metaphysical empire does not necessarily have to end with a verdict that either mutual exclusivists are right and cultural appropriationists are wrong or cultural appropriationists are right and mutual exclusivists are wrong because, to reiterate, things are not always either/or. Things are either/or if the options are A and non-A; that is if one is necessarily correct, the other being the opposite must be necessarily wrong. But if the options are A, B, they can be neither/nor if both are wrong, but it can also be A and B if both are right. Furthermore, either of them can be fully or partially right or wrong. So things can also be partially A and partially B, partially A and fully B, or fully A and partially B (Abumere, 2015, 2022).

There is nothing in the metaphysical empire debate to suggest that the relationship between mutual exclusivism and cultural appropriationism is that of A and non-A. Consequently, there is nothing in the debate to suggest that if mutual exclusivists are necessarily right, then cultural appropriationists must be necessarily wrong and vice versa. Furthermore, it is evident that I do not think that we should 'totally' jettison the views of both mutual exclusivists and cultural appropriationists (seeing the views as totally wrong) or 'totally' embrace the views (seeing the views as totally right). And I do not think one is fully right while the other is partially right or one is fully wrong while the other is partially wrong. As my accommodative decolonisation suggests, I see both mutual exclusivists and cultural appropriationists to be partially right and partially wrong.

Consequently, I propose fusion of horizons as the way forward for the discourse on the metaphysical empire. Nevertheless, I am conscious that 'fusion of horizons is not a quick fix' (Abumere, 2015, p. 36) because mutual exclusivists think that they are totally right and cultural appropriationists are totally wrong, while cultural appropriationists also think that they are totally right and mutual exclusivists are totally wrong. These absolutist positions taken by both mutual exclusivists and cultural appropriationists are not surprising because,

> naturally, given our high valuation of our stance, we would like to hold on to our stance even when rigorously challenged. It is only when we humbly realise that our stance is not, or should not be, absolute that we begin to entertain the possibility of fusion of horizons.
>
> (Abumere, 2015, p. 36)

The same way 'our stance is not or should not be absolute, so too the other's stance is not or should not be absolute' (Abumere, 2015, p. 36). Therefore, when we are invited to fuse our horizon with the horizon of another person,

> we are not invited to jettison our stance for the other's stance, just as we are not asked to jettison the other's stance for ours. We are only asked to fuse the two stances. Here it is assumed that both stances are not so absurd that they are worthless. They are assumed to be reasonable to the extent that there are plausible and positive elements within them that are worthwhile fusing.
>
> (p. 36)

In our journey to fusion of horizons, our endeavour to arrive at a robust comprehension of our subject matter

> always involves rising to a higher universality that overcomes not only our own particularity but also that of the other. The concept of 'horizon' suggests itself because it expresses the superior breadth of vision that the person who is trying to understand must have. To acquire a horizon means that one learns to look beyond what is close at hand – not in order to look away from it but to see it better, within a larger whole and in truer proportion.
>
> (Gadamer, 1992, p. 305) (emphasis in original)

As the name makes explicit, fusion of horizons as a concept combines two sub-concepts, namely fusion and horizon. In everyday language, horizon is the physical limit of our vision while fusion has to do with combining plural or multiple things in order to make them a singular unit. While my adoption of fusion of horizons resonates with the everyday language sense of horizon and fusion, it does not exactly denote such everyday language usage. I am interested in a philosophical use of fusion of horizons. Consequently, I adopt the Gadamerian philosophical usage of fusion of horizons.

Although Hans-Georg Gadamer (1989) is not the originator of the concept of fusion of horizons and the philosophical use, he 'is rightly notable for his use of the concept as the pivot of his hermeneutics' (Abumere, 2015, pp. 36–38). Like Gadamer (1989), I see fusion of horizons as a hermeneutic for the interpretation of texts. But for the purposes of the metaphysical empire, I go beyond narrowly seeing fusion of horizons as a hermeneutic for the interpretation of texts to broadly seeing it as a value-neutral hermeneutical device for the resolution of opposition views in a philosophical debate. In this sense,

> I am not following Gadamer dogmatically .... In this case, although my use of the concept is an extension of Gadamer's, the proper way to understand my use of the concept is to note the following. My use is flexible rather than rigid. It is an adaptation rather than the original. Most importantly, it is an application rather than a transfer or transposition, and a conversion rather than a transportation, of Gadamer's fusion of horizons.
>
> (Abumere, 2015, pp. 36–38)

I opt for a flexible use, adaptation and application of fusion of horizons in order to use the strengths of mutual exclusivism to compensate for the weaknesses of cultural appropriationism, and to use the strengths of cultural appropriationism to compensate for the weaknesses of mutual exclusivism. For the purpose of my applied use,

> I tilt Gadamer's fusion of horizons from hermeneutics to [... the metaphysical empire] in the following way. I am not using it as a mere hermeneutic theory of interpretation which is primarily aimed at helping us conduct dialogues and which sees a 'successful' dialogue as an end in itself.
>
> (pp. 36–38)

Therefore, the fusion of the horizons of mutual exclusivism and cultural appropriationism 'is not an end in itself but a means to' (pp. 36–38) arrive at a realistic resolution to the problem of the metaphysical empire.

I must clarify that my fusion of the horizons of mutual exclusivism and cultural appropriationism

> is not Hegelian dialectics of, say, being + nothingness = becoming, or thesis + antithesis = synthesis which itself becomes a new thesis. Nevertheless, fusion of horizons occurs when individuals understand that the context of their discourse can be seen from a different perspective in order to reach a new conclusion.
>
> (Abumere, 2015, p. 193; see Vessey, n.d., s.p.)

My fusion of the horizons of mutual exclusivists and cultural appropriationists presupposes that both the former and the latter already have horizons. Taking a cue from Gadamer (1989), I think that it is important to have a horizon because 'a person who has no horizon does not see far enough and hence overvalues what is nearest to him' (p. 302). But I admit that Eric Donald Hirsch Jr. (1967)'s criticism of fusion of horizons may make one 'think twice' before adopting the Gadamerian fusion of horizons because the criticism is the most important criticism – at least in my opinion – that one must consider before adopting fusion of horizons.

Hirsch Jr. (1967) is of the opinion that fusion of horizons, as Gadamer conceptualises it, does not leave any room for horizons to be fused. For him, in fact, it is impossible to fuse horizons within the framework of Gadamer's conception of the concept. He argues that

> it is impossible for a person to fuse her own horizon and that of the text together. For such a fusion to happen, she must have understood the original perspective of the text and integrate it into her own perspective. Given that fusion of horizons cannot happen without her understanding the original perspective of the text, and given that once she understands the original perspective of the text it is automatically no longer beyond her horizon, then fusion of horizons is impossible.
>
> (Abumere, 2015, p. 37)

The crux of the problem Hirsch Jr. has with Gadamer and Gadamer's conceptualisation of fusion of horizons, and the crux of Hirsch Jr.'s argument is that,

> if the original perspective of the text is beyond our horizon, then we cannot understand the text. If this is the case, then fusion of horizons is impossible. As long as we are limited by our own horizon, then we cannot break the barrier of this limitedness in order to fuse our horizon with that of the text. Saying that we can break the barrier of this limitedness in order to fuse our horizon with the text is tantamount to saying that we were not in the first place limited at all. If so, then there was no horizon in the first place.
>
> (Abumere, 2015, p. 37; see Hirsch Jr., 1967, p. 254)

Hirsch Jr.'s criticism is not trivial; it is serious. Thus it should be taken seriously. However, as I explained elsewhere, his criticism would have been apt if, and only if, 'Gadamer used horizon in the ordinary language sense of the word' (Abumere, 2015, p. 27). Gadamer did not use horizons in the ordinary language sense. Following in the footsteps of Edmund Husserl (1931) and taking his cue and drawing insights from Husserl's phenomenology,

> Gadamer reconceptualised horizon to play a [philosophical…] role in his hermeneutics. Like Husserl, Gadamer did not lay emphasis on the meaning of horizon as a limit. Rather, he emphasised horizon as that which we can enlarge, as that which gives us pointers to something else and somewhere else and as that which we can go outside of in order to reach some new place.
>
> (Abumere, 2015, p. 27)

After all, as Jeff Malpas (2009) says,

> the 'horizon' is the larger context of meaning in which any particular meaningful presentation is situated. Inasmuch as understanding is taken to involve a 'fusion of horizons,' then so it always involves the formation of a new context of meaning that enables integration of what is otherwise unfamiliar, strange or anomalous. In this respect, all understanding involves a process of mediation and dialogue between what is familiar and what is alien in which neither remains unaffected.
>
> (s.p.) (emphasis in original)

Therefore, in spite of the fact that 'horizon designates our particular limit at a particular time and place, it does not confine us to that limit. It leaves us the opportunity to walk ahead and see further' (Abumere, 2015, pp. 36–38; see Vessey, n.d.). It is for this reason that Gadamer (1992) asserts that 'real fusing of horizons ... means that as the historical horizon is projected, it is simultaneously superseded' (p. 307).

Fusion of Horizons

In the preceding sub-chapter, I briefly presented a preview of how Gadamer (1989, 1992) conceptualised fusion of horizons in his hermeneutic and I explained how I am adopting and adapting it for the purposes of my accommodative decolonisation. The implication of predicating my accommodative decolonisation on Gadamerian fusion of horizons is that if Gadamer is wrong then I am wrong, and if he is right then I may be right. Consequently, in this sub-chapter, I shall explicate Gadamer's fusion of horizons in detail in order for us to see its plausibility and by extension, the plausibility of accommodative decolonisation.

Gadamer (1992), first and foremost, asserts that 'hermeneutical consciousness is involved neither with technical nor moral knowledge' (p. 315). Moreover, he clarifies that his 'real concern was and is philosophic: not what we do or what we ought to do, but what happens to us over and above our wanting and doing' (p. 28). According to Gadamer (1997), 'hermeneutic philosophy understands itself not as an absolute position but as a way of experience. It insists that there is no higher principle than holding oneself open in a conversation' (p. 189).

Furthermore, Gadamer explains that he understands hermeneutics as the capacity of the self 'to listen to the other in the belief that the other could be right' (qtd. in Grondin & Plant, 2003, p. 250). This demonstrates why he is focused on dialogue. Looking at his hermeneutics, you will see that the concept of fusion of horizons is a derivative of Gadamer's account of dialogue. In his account of dialogue, Gadamer (1992) says that 'to reach an understanding in a dialogue is not merely a matter of putting oneself forward and successfully asserting one's own point of view, but being transformed into a communion in which we do not remain what we were' (p. 379).

In the aforementioned account of dialogue, two things are noticeable. First, a reader has the possibility of dialoguing, and has both the capacity and room to dialogue, with the text she reads. Second, 'dialogue represents an active language or a language in action; and the fusion of horizons is the end result of any successful dialogue' (Abumere, 2015, pp. 36–38; see Vessey, n.d.). For the aforementioned reasons, Gadamer (1992) explains that

> what I described as a fusion of horizons was the form in which this unity actualises itself, which does not allow the interpreter to speak of an original meaning of the work without acknowledging that, in

> understanding it, the interpreter's own meaning enters in as well …. Working out the historical horizon of a text is always already a fusion of horizons.
>
> (pp. 576, 577)

As already mentioned, Gadamer's fusion of horizons and hermeneutics can be traced to Husserl's phenomenology. But we have to go through Martin Heidegger's phenomenology. Although Gadamer's focus on linguistics is a noticeable and important deviation from Husserl's focus on perception (Vessey, n.d.), what I think is more noticeable and important is that Gadamer, basing his hermeneutics on the phenomenology of his predecessors namely Husserl and Heidegger, thinks that fusion of horizons is the best way for a reader to dialogue with the text she reads or for parties in a conversation to dialogue with each other (Abumere, 2015).

In terms of the relationship between his fusion of horizons and Husserl's phenomenology, Gadamer (1989) states:

> Undoubtedly the concept and phenomenon of the horizon is of crucial importance for Husserl's phenomenological research. With this concept … Husserl is obviously seeking to capture the way all limited intentionality of meaning merges into the fundamental continuity of the whole. A horizon is not a rigid boundary but something that moves with one and invites one to advance further. Thus the horizon intentionality that constitutes the unity of the flow of experience is paralleled by an equally comprehensive horizon intentionality on the objective side. For everything that is given as existent is given in terms of a world and thus the world horizon is given with it.
>
> (p. 245)

Gadamer's claim about Husserl's phenomenology, particularly the Husserlian conception of horizon, is accurate because Husserl (1931) himself argues that

> perception has horizons made up of other possibilities of perception, as perceptions we could have, if we actively directed the course of perception otherwise: if, for example, we turned our eyes that way instead of this, or if we were to step forward or to one side, and so forth.
>
> (p. 44)

To properly understand the Husserlian conception of horizon, we need to understand that, for Husserl:

> there are three types of horizons, namely; internal horizon, external horizon and temporal horizon. Internal horizons are those characteristics

> that an object necessarily has because they are in the nature of the object. External horizons are those horizons that establish the relationship between an object and its environment. Temporal horizons denote the temporal nature or circumstances of the object. In other words, the internal horizon denotes the existence of the object – its nature. The external horizon denotes the special relations of the object to the environment. Whereas the temporal horizon, cum the internal and external horizons, denotes the spatio-temporal nature of the object and its relations to time, space, other objects and its environment.
>
> (Abumere, 2015, pp. 36–38; see Vessey, n.d.)

Although Husserl values the three types of horizon, he thinks that temporal horizon is more valuable than both internal and external horizons. For him, temporal horizon is the most valuable horizon because he thinks that

> we see all objects as temporal objects, as objects that are not only extended in space but also in time. Given that the inner horizon is made known to us by our common expectations of future disclosures about the object, and given that the outer horizon is made known to us as how the object relates to its surroundings, therefore temporality is the vital link between objects and other horizons.
>
> (Abumere, 2015, pp. 36–38; see Vessey, n.d.)

Temporality or time is essential in the conception of horizon and temporal horizon is the most valuable horizon for Husserl because he thinks that

> future disclosures and relations, including the history of the object that made the object the sort of object that it is and put it in the place where it is, are in essence temporal. Hence, he argues that it is the temporal horizon that makes other horizons possible.
>
> (Abumere, 2015, pp. 36–38; see Vessey, n.d.)

Similar to Husserl's claim about temporal horizon, Heidegger (1996) claims that time is 'the possible horizon for any understanding of being' (p. 19). Horizon, for Heidegger (1982), is 'that towards which each *ecstasis* is intrinsically open in a specific way … the open expanse towards which remotion itself is outside itself' (p. 267). The line of thought from Husserl through Heidegger to Gadamer becomes very clear when Gadamer (1997) explains that the purpose of his hermeneutic is an endeavour 'to take up and elaborate this line of thinking from the later Heidegger' (p. 47). The similarity between Heidegger's thought and Gadamer's thought is especially noticeable when we juxtapose the former's idea of *ecstasis* with the latter's claim that 'understanding is made possible because thinking continuously "points beyond itself"'(Gadamer, 1989, p. 186) (emphasis in original).

However, nearly four decades after the publication of his magnus opus *Truth and Method*, Gadamer (1997) turned around to argue that defending the importance of temporal distance is neither valuable for the defence of the importance of 'the otherness of the other' (p. 45) nor valuable for the defence of 'the essential role that language plays as conversation' (Abumere, 2015, pp. 36–38; see Gadamer, 1997, p. 45). As far as he is concerned,

> interpretive distance needs not always be a historical distance, and it is not always temporal distance that helps us defeat erroneous memories and images and their resonance and warped uses. But temporal distance is still very helpful because it is only through temporal distance that certain changes are made apparent to us and certain differences become observable.
>
> (Abumere, 2015, pp. 36–38; see Gadamer, 1997, p. 45)

From Husserl, to Heidegger, to Gadamer, we can deduce the importance of horizon for the debate on the metaphysical empire. Mutual exclusivism is one horizon and cultural appropriationism is another horizon. The problem in the metaphysical empire debate is that both mutual exclusivists and cultural appropriationists do not see beyond their respective horizons. The failure to see beyond one's horizon is a limitation that can only be overcome when one fuses her horizon with the horizon of the other. As Gadamer (1989) says, horizon is limiting because it is 'the range of vision that includes everything that can be seen from a particular vantage point' (p. 302).

It is important that mutual exclusivists and cultural appropriationists have horizons because 'a person who has no horizon does not see far enough and hence overvalues what is nearest to him' (p. 302). However, it is more important that they engage in fusion of horizons because 'every finite present has its limitations. We define the concept of "situation" by saying that it represents a standpoint that limits the possibility of vision. Hence essential to the concept of a situation is the concept of a "horizon"' (p. 302) (emphasis in original).

Consequently, the simple act of a mutual exclusivist or a cultural appropriationist changing her standpoint causes her to have 'the possibility of having different horizons' because the simple act of 'stepping out of our horizons entails the possibility of having broader horizons' (Abumere, 2015, pp. 36–38). After all, in its philosophical sense, 'horizon entails the possibility of the gradual expansion of our range of vision' (pp. 36–38). Therefore, horizon prevents us from being 'limited by what is nearby, but to see beyond it' (Gadamer, 1989, p. 302).

According to Gadamer (1992), 'in understanding we are drawn into an event of truth and arrive, as it were, too late, if we want to know what we are supposed to believe' (p. 490). Moreover, the hallmark of horizon is 'flexibility rather than rigidity … rather than being a non-shifting border line, horizon actually shifts with us and encourages us to go forward' (Abumere, 2015, p. 36–38; see Gadamer, 1989, p. 245). In the final analysis, Gadamer (1989) asserts that

> the historical movement of human life consists in the fact that it is never absolutely bound to any one standpoint, and hence can never have a truly closed horizon. The horizon is, rather, something into which we move and that moves with us. Horizons change for someone who is moving.
>
> (p. 304)

To summarise the foregoing discussion on fusion of horizons, I would say that fusion of horizons is best understood by noticing what it rejects. There are three key rejections that are associated with fusion of horizons. Firstly, it 'simultaneously rejects objectivism and universalism' (Abumere, 2015, p. 36). Secondly, 'it rejects objectivism whereby the self objectifies the other's horizon and discounts the self's or at the expense of the self's' (p. 36). Thirdly, 'it rejects universalism whereby a singular horizon is the sole holder of the truth, the whole truth and nothing but the whole truth' (p. 36). Based on these three rejections, fusion of horizons concludes that 'we are not closed-up in a closed horizon' (p. 36).

As earlier mentioned, 'fusion of horizons is not Hegelian dialectics of, say, being + nothingness = becoming or thesis + antithesis = synthesis which itself becomes a new thesis' (p. 36). However, fusion of horizons happens when parties in a conversation realise that it is possible to view the context of their conversation 'from a different perspective in order to reach a new conclusion' (Abumere, 2015, p. 36; see Vessey, n.d.). For this reason,

> The acquisition of novel information, or the development of a novel perception of the existing information, makes individuals re-evaluate their previous conclusions, make individuals aware of the limitations of their previous conclusions, help individuals gain a novel understanding of their discourse, and supposedly leads to a fusion of the horizons of the individuals who are involved in the discourse.
>
> (Abumere, 2015, p. 36; see Vessey, n.d.)

Therefore, at least four things will happen: First, the limitations of prior conclusions will be minimised; second, prior understanding will be improved; third, novel perspectives will be formed; and fourth, the previously limited horizon will become a broadened horizon (Abumere, 2015, p. 36; see Vessey, n.d.). This is why Gadamer (1989) says that 'it requires a special effort to acquire a historical horizon' (p. 305). In the metaphysical empire debate, it is such effort that is required of mutual exclusivists and cultural appropriationists.

A Recapitulation

As I reach the end of this concluding chapter and the entire book, I will conclude the chapter and the book by recapitulating the discussion in the book and by reiterating my argument. In the introductory chapter, I explained what the metaphysical empire is, and what its scope and content are. In a novel way, I juxtaposed the physical empire with the metaphysical empire, extended the domain of the metaphysical empire beyond its usual linguistic domain, and preliminarily explored the place of the metaphysical empire in the decolonisation project and the extent to which the project should or should not be concerned with the metaphysical empire. Then, by way of conclusion, I explained that the preliminary discussion in the chapter will be explored in detail in the subsequent chapters.

In the second chapter, based on the preliminary exploration in the introductory chapter, I engaged in an advanced exploration of the debate between cultural appropriationists and mutual exclusivists. I explained that the former think that we can appropriate colonial heritage such as the English language and use it as if it were part and parcel of the African culture, and that this is in no way antithetical to decolonisation. But the latter argue that authentic decolonisation entails that we must completely dissociate the African and her culture from colonial heritage.

The English, French, Portuguese, Spanish, German and Afrikaans (South African version of Dutch) languages in Africa are relics of colonialism, and as such, are residual colonialism. Being residual colonialism, for mutual exclusivists, these languages are part and parcel of the metaphysical empire. Consequently, in the post-colony, to hold on to these White and European languages which were used in the colony and not to return to the African languages of the pre-colony is to allow oneself to be subjected to the metaphysical empire and consent to be a subject of the metaphysical empire.

In the second chapter, I delved into the aforementioned debate by, on the one hand, exploring the strengths and weaknesses of cultural appropriationism and, on the other hand, testing the validity of mutual exclusivism. In view of the limitations of both the former and the latter, I concluded that neither the former nor the latter is qualified to be taken as the canonical position on the subject of the metaphysical empire. But in view of their strengths, I also concluded that we need to balance the views of both the former and the latter in order to be able to navigate the murky waters of the metaphysical empire.

In the third chapter, I stated that since racial identity in particular and identity in general are the principal determinants of where Africans stand on the question of the metaphysical empire and the decolonisation debate, it is important that I explain my conception of both the concept of race and the concept of identity. This explanation was the subject matter of the chapter – in the subsequent chapters, I explained why and how the concepts of race and identity play key roles in the enduring legacies of colonialism which are simultaneously manifested and reflected in ongoing-colonialism, that is, a combination of colonialism, neocolonialism and the metaphysical empire.

Essentially, in the third chapter, I revisited the conceptual and theoretical framework of the book, which revolves around the phenomenon of identity. I introduced and explicated the phenomenon in both its narrow sense (racial identity) and broad sense in order to prepare the grounds for the discussion in the remainder of the book. Based on the preliminary discussion of the phenomenon of identity in the chapter, I engaged in a detailed analysis of the implications of this phenomenon for the debate on the metaphysical empire in the remainder of the book. To this effect, I divided the discussion in the chapter into two parts. In the first part, I briefly teased out the concept of race. In the second part, I explained the concept of identity, the kind of identity I am concerned about and how this in turn informs the value that mutual exclusivists place on racial identity.

Having explained what the metaphysical empire is in the introductory chapter, having resolved the quandary between cultural appropriationism and mutual exclusivism in the second chapter, and following my discussion in the third chapter in which I explained the key role of the concept of identity (and the concept of racial identity) in the metaphysical empire debate, in the fourth chapter – taking a cue from Kwasi Wiredu – I drew insights from metaphysics to simultaneously delineate the (metaphorical) boundaries of the metaphysical empire and tease out the grounds on which African cultures can appropriate some useful aspects of Western cultures without the danger of falling into the metaphysical empire.

Like Wiredu (1997), I confronted 'the paradox that while Western cultures recoil from claims of universality, previously colonised peoples, seeking to redefine their identities, insist on cultural particularities' (s.p.).[1] And like him, I thought that 'universals, rightly conceived on the basis of our common biological identity, are not incompatible with cultural particularities and, in fact, are what make intercultural communication possible' (Wiredu, 1997, s.p.).[2]

My discussion on cultural universals and cultural particulars in the fourth chapter demonstrated that cultural appropriation without the danger of falling into the metaphysical empire is possible. But this poses a problem for the decolonisation project, namely where does decolonisation begin and end or where should the project start and stop. In view of this dilemma, in the fifth chapter, I explored different pertinent issues such as theoretical plausibility versus practicable possibility (what may be possible in theory but not in practice in the decolonisation project?); theoretical imperative versus practical necessity (what does decolonisation require both in theory and in practice vis-à-vis the metaphysical empire?); and the authenticity argument (that is, returning to and retaining original African languages) versus the efficiency argument (that is, easier to appropriate and use Western languages).

In the fifth chapter, I argued that what the dilemma of decolonisation demonstrates is that even in the face of the danger of the metaphysical empire, the decolonisation project can still be accommodative. An accommodative decolonisation, recognising the relationship between cultural universals and cultural particulars, simultaneously promotes the originality and authenticity of African cultures and creates room for cultural appropriation because it sees certain things as human achievement rather than African, European, American, Asian, Arabic or Chinese achievement.

Finally – in view of the discussion in the introductory, first, second, third, fourth and fifth chapters, and in view of my argument in the discussion – in this concluding chapter I argued that both cultural appropriationists and mutual exclusivists must simultaneously renounce absolutism (this does not mean they should embrace relativism) and be amenable to fusion of horizons. Consequently, I proposed fusion of horizons as the way forward for the discourse on the metaphysical empire.

I explained that by arguing that both cultural appropriationists and mutual exclusivists must simultaneously renounce absolutism (this does not mean they should embrace relativism) and be amenable to fusion of horizons, and by proposing fusion of horizons as the way forward for the discourse on the metaphysical empire, I avoided what I referred to as the decolonisation fallacy which is tantamount to arguing that things are always either/or.

To reiterate, things are not always either/or. Things are either/or if the options are A and non-A; that is if one is necessarily correct, the other being the logical opposite must be necessarily wrong. But if the options are A, B, they can be neither/nor if both are wrong, but it can also be A and B if both are right. Furthermore, either of them can be fully or partially right or wrong. So things can also be partially A and partially B, partially A and fully B, or fully A and partially B (Abumere, 2015).

To summarise – in the context of the metaphysical empire debate and in view of the disagreement between mutual exclusivists and cultural appropriationists – in this concluding chapter, taking a cue from Gadamer (1989), I argued that it is important to have a horizon because 'a person who has no horizon does not see far enough and hence overvalues what is nearest to him' (p. 302). I clarified that

> fusion of horizons is not Hegelian dialectics of, say, being + nothingness = becoming, or thesis + antithesis = synthesis which itself becomes a new thesis. Nevertheless, fusion of horizons occurs when individuals understand that the context of their discourse can be seen from a different perspective in order to reach a new conclusion.
>
> (Abumere, 2015, p. 193; see Vessey, n.d., s.p.)

The essence of my accommodative decolonisation – qualified decolonisation or decolonisation with a caveat – is to get mutual exclusivists and cultural appropriationists to understand that the context of the metaphysical empire discourse can be seen from a different perspective. When they see the context of the metaphysical empire discourse from a different perspective, then they will reach a new conclusion. And if they reach a new conclusion, then fusion of horizons would have occurred.

Notes

1 See the description on the cover page of *Cultural Universals and Particulars: An African Perspective*. See Bibliography for full details.
2 See the description on the cover page of *Cultural Universals and Particulars: An African Perspective*. See Bibliography for full details.

Bibliography

Abumere, F. A. (2015) *Different Perspectives on Global Justice: A Fusion of Horizons*. Bielefeld, Publication at Bielefeld University (PUB).

Abumere, F. A. (2022) *Global Justice and Resource Curse: Combining Statism and Cosmopolitanism*. London, Routledge.

Abumere, F. A. (2023) *African Identities and International Politics*. London, Routledge.

Gadamer, H.-G. (1989) *Truth and Method*. New York, Crossroad.

Gadamer, H.-G. (1992) In: Weinsheimer, J. & Marshall, D. G. (trans.) *Truth and Method*, 2nd ed. New York, Crossroad.

Gadamer, H-G. (1997) Reflections on my philosophical journey. In: Hahn, L. E. (ed.) *The Philosophy of Hans-Georg Gadamer*. Peru, IL, Open Court, pp. 3–63.

Grondin, J. & Plant, K. (2003) *The Philosophy of Gadamer*. London, Routledge.

Heidegger, M. (1982) *The Basic Problems of Phenomenology*. Bloomington, IN, Indiana University Press.

Heidegger, M. (1996) *Being and Time*. Stambuagh, J. (trans.). Albany, NY, SUNY Press.

Hirsch, Jr., E. D. (1967) *Validity in Interpretation*. New Haven, CT, Yale University Press.

Husserl, E. (1931[1973]) *Cartesian Meditations*. Den Hague, Martinus Nijhoff.

Malpas J. (2009) Hans-Georg Gadamer. *The Stanford Encyclopedia of Philosophy*, Spring ed. https://plato.stanford.edu/archives/spr2009/entries/gadamer/

Mignolo, W. D. (2011) *The Darker Side of Western Modernity: Global Futures, Decolonial Options*. Durham, NC, Duke University Press.

Ndlovu-Gatsheni, S. J. (2018) Metaphysical empire, linguicides and cultural imperialism. *English Academy Review* 35 (2), 96 – 115.

Vessey, D. (n.d.) Gadamer and the fusion of horizons. www.davevessey.com/gadamer_Horizons.htm

Wa Thiong'o, N. (1993) *Moving the Centre: The Struggle for Cultural Freedoms*. Oxford, James Currey.

Wiredu, K. (1995) The concept of mind with particular references to the language and thought of the Akan. In: Kwame, S. (ed.) *Readings in African Philosophy: An Akan Collection*. Lanham, MD, University Press of America, pp. 120–136.

Wiredu, K. (1997) *Cultural Universals and Particulars: An African Perspective*. Bloomington, IN, Indiana University Press.

Index

For Product Safety Concerns and Information please contact our EU representative GPSR@taylorandfrancis.com
Taylor & Francis Verlag GmbH, Kaufingerstraße 24, 80331 München, Germany

www.ingramcontent.com/pod-product-compliance
Lightning Source LLC
LaVergne TN
LVHW010930110826
845149LV00013B/2532
* 9 7 8 1 0 3 2 9 6 5 4 1 3 *